THE WESTERN FRONTIER LIBRARY

Henry A. Wallace's Irrigation Frontier

Henry A. Wallace's, *1888-1965* Irrigation Frontier,

Agard

On the Trail of the Corn Belt Farmer, 1909

Edited and with an Introduction by

Richard Lowitt and Judith Fabry

University of Oklahoma : Norman and London

Other Books by Richard Lowitt

Merchant Prince of the Nineteenth Century: William E. Dodge
(New York, 1954)
George W. Norris: The Making of a Progressive, 1861–1912
(Syracuse, N.Y., 1963)
(ed.) *The Truman-MacArthur Controversy* (Chicago, 1967)
George W. Norris: The Persistence of a Progressive, 1912–1933
(Champaign, Ill., 1971)
(coed.) *Interpreting Twentieth-Century America* (New York, 1973)
George W. Norris: The Triumph of a Progressive, 1933–1944
(Champaign, Ill., 1978)
(ed.) *The Journal of a Tamed Bureaucrat: Nils Olsen and the B.A.E.*
(Ames, Iowa, 1980)
(coed.) *One Third of a Nation: Lorena Hickok Reports on the Great
Depression* (Champaign, Ill., 1981)
The New Deal and the West (Bloomington, Ind., 1984)
(coed.) *Letters of an American Farmer: Eastern European Correspondence of
Roswell Garst* (De Kalb, Ill., 1986)

Library of Congress Cataloging-in-Publication Data

Wallace, Henry Agard, 1888–1965.
    Henry A. Wallace's irrigation frontier : On the trail of the corn
belt farmer, 1909 / edited and with an introduction by Richard
Lowitt and Judith Fabry.
        p.   cm.—(The Western frontier library : 58)
    Includes index.
    ISBN 0-8061-2332-X
    1. Irrigation farming—West (U.S.)   2. Irrigation—West (U.S.)
    3. Agriculture—West (U.S.)   4. Wallace, Henry Agard, 1888–1965—
Journeys—West (U.S.)   5. West (U.S.)—Description and
travel—1880–1950.   I. Lowitt, Richard, 1922–   II. Fabry,
Judith K.   III. Title.   IV. Series.
S616.U6W35   1991
631.5'87'0975—dc20   91-8976
                                                                     CIP

Copyright © 1991 by the University of Oklahoma Press, Norman, Publishing Division
of the University. All rights reserved. Manufactured in the U.S.A. First edition.

Henry A. Wallace's Irrigation Frontier: On the Trail of the Corn Belt Farmer, 1909
is Volume 58 in The Western Frontier Library.

Contents

Contents

Illustrations

Acknowledgments

For assistance in transcribing the articles we are indebted to Audrey Burton, and for general assistance, as always, to Carole Kennedy—the secretary serving the Department of History at Iowa State University. It was a paper prepared by Richard S. Kirkendall—first presented at a seminar he sponsored, and later discussed by the Vigilantes, an informal Iowa State History Department group—that prompted us to investigate his brief references to the stories Henry A. Wallace filed. Professor Kirkendall is preparing an intellectual biography of Henry A. Wallace.

Richard Lowitt
Judith Fabry

Henry A. Wallace's Irrigation Frontier

Henry A. Wallace, 1910

Introduction

This introduction is divided into two parts. The first examines the author of the articles, Henry Agard Wallace, within a biographical context. He was the third Henry in a distinguished Iowa family committed to furthering the perceived virtues of rural living and country life through education and journalism. It was in this capacity as a rising senior at Iowa State College (ISC) and as a reporter on assignment for the family journal, *Wallaces' Farmer,* that he went west in 1909. The second part examines the state of irrigation agriculture in the United States at that time. Aside from a foray into Texas, farming, primarily irrigation agriculture and only briefly dry farming, commanded Wallace's attention. The first article was published in the July 2, 1909, issue of *Wallaces' Farmer,* the last in the issue of March 18, 1910. Some were written during his summer travels; most were published in the course of his final year as an animal husbandry major at Iowa State College.

Henry A. Wallace

As twenty-one-year-old Henry Agard Wallace traveled through the West, he recorded information and impressions while visiting with farmers and their families in new and developing agricultural areas, including the federal irrigation projects. He was "On the Trail of the Corn Belt Farmer," seeking to learn how transplanted midwesterners were faring in their ventures into irrigated or dryland farming.

Wallace's interest in and knowledge of agriculture and rural life had deep roots. He was the son of Henry C. Wallace and the grandson of Henry Wallace, who in 1909 were the editors of *Wallaces' Farmer,* a prestigious Iowa-based farm journal. Before becoming full-time journalists, both father and grandfather had been engaged in scientific, commercial and experimental farming. The elder Wallace, who had been a Presbyterian minister for several years before taking up farming, was a deeply religious man with strongly held beliefs that rural life embodied and preserved the moral values most fundamental to the continued well-being of American society. Through their farm journal the Wallaces hoped to influence American farmers to adopt scientific methods of farming that would permit them to prosper, remain on the land, and create attractive and dynamic rural communities.

Henry A. Wallace, the observant and articulate young man who toured the West in 1909, had been born in 1888, the first of six children of Henry C. and May Broadhead Wallace. At the time of his birth, his parents lived in Adair County, Iowa, where they rented a farm belonging to Henry Wallace. Three years earlier Henry C. had begun the agricultural course at ISC, but had dropped out soon after because he was "bored and in love."[1] When a reorganization of the agricultural curriculum took place in 1891, Henry C. was motivated to move his small family to Ames

---

[1] " 'Chip of the Old Block,' " *News of Iowa State* 18 (March–April 1966), pages unnumbered.

and return to school. He completed the course in a year and then joined the staff of the college's agricultural experiment station.

During the years when his family lived in Ames, young Henry A. began developing what would become a life-long interest in plants and plant breeding. George Washington Carver, who was a student at ISC during this period, became a friend of the Wallaces and took a special liking to the small boy. Henry A. sometimes accompanied Carver on his botanizing expeditions, learning from his mentor to identify plant parts and observing how fertilization occurred. At the age of eight, under his mother's supervision, Henry A. conducted his first effort at plant cross-breeding, using pansies for his subjects.[2]

The years in Ames also marked the beginning of the Wallace family's journalistic enterprise. During the early 1880s, having made a name for himself in his local paper by writing a regular column about agricultural issues, the senior Henry Wallace had begun an editorial association with the influential *Iowa Homestead*. In its columns he continued to discuss agricultural problems and became known for his no-nonsense stands that were free of political bias. In 1894, however, Wallace's unwillingness to bend to the political opinions of the owners of the *Homestead* cost him his position. Shortly before this time, Henry C. Wallace had purchased a part-interest in another Iowa farm journal, *The Farm and Dairy*. In 1895, recognizing the important role

---

[2] Transcript, "The Reminiscences of Henry Agard Wallace," vol. 1, 1888–1934, compiled 1950–51 by the Oral History Research Office of Columbia University, 4.

the senior Wallace played in the agricultural development of the state and that he would not be content for long without a forum in which to express his opinions, Henry C. and his brother, John, purchased *The Farm and Dairy* outright and asked their father to become the editor. A year later the family moved their journalistic operation from Ames to Des Moines and changed the name of the publication to *Wallaces' Farmer*. Their paper rapidly increased in popularity and its circulation spread to the surrounding states. By the turn of the century, the wisdom of the weekly editorials and sabbath school lessons of Henry Wallace had become legendary and had made "Uncle Henry," as he was affectionately known to readers and friends, a regular part of the lives of many midwestern and western farm families.[3]

By 1896 it was apparent that the influence and reputation of Henry Wallace was not limited to the Midwest, but extended all the way to Washington, D.C. Following his election, President William McKinley suggested that Henry Wallace might become his secretary of agriculture. Although Wallace declined the offer, he recommended an old friend from Iowa, James ("Tama Jim") Wilson, for the position. McKinley followed his advice, and Wilson accepted the position, which he held until 1913.

A decade later, President Theodore Roosevelt invited Henry Wallace to be a member of the newly formed Country Life Commission. Roosevelt established the commission in 1907 because he and concerned urban agrarians

[3] Edward L. and Frederick H. Schapsmeier, *Henry A. Wallace of Iowa: The Agrarian Years, 1910–1940* (Ames: Iowa State University Press, 1968), 9.

had determined that rural living standards and social achievements lagged behind those of American cities and were the result of an inefficient and poorly organized rural economy. Since it seemed clear that the urban-industrial sector could not prosper without a healthy rural sector, Roosevelt proposed that the commission survey rural life in America and make recommendations about how it could be revolutionized to bring it up to urban standards. In 1908, as a member of the commission, Henry Wallace participated in a tour of the nation's agricultural regions and helped prepare the report that described the economic and social problems of the farm families they had observed. Among the other members of the commission were Liberty Hyde Bailey, Kenyon L. Butterfield, and Gifford Pinchot.[4]

Henry A. Wallace was growing up while his grandfather gained national prominence as a spokesman for agriculture and rural life, and his father and uncle worked to make *Wallaces' Farmer* a prominent and profitable farm journal. He went to public schools, worked in the family's garden and orchard, took care of their farm animals, and learned about agriculture from his father and grandfather. The practical experience he obtained was balanced and enhanced by his grandfather's continuing interest in agricultural experimentation. "Uncle Henry" had traded his farm in Adair County for another that was closer to Des Moines. Young Henry accompanied his grandfather on trips to

---

[4] David B. Danbom, *The Resisted Revolution: Urban America and the Industrialization of Agriculture, 1900–1930* (Ames: Iowa State University Press, 1979), 42–44. Danbom provides a brief but insightful summary of the work of the Country Life Commission and also places the commission and the Country Life movement in the context of Progressive reform.

inspect the farm and learned about the experiments he was conducting there. In later years Henry A. concluded that his grandfather seldom profited directly from his on-the-land experiments, but profited indirectly, by writing about them.[5]

By the time he had reached high school, Henry A. had established himself as a solid student, but he failed to measure up to what he perceived to be the aristocratic social standards of West Des Moines High School. Agricultural problems, instead of relations with his peers, absorbed the young Wallace. During his high school years he conducted a corn-growing experiment to test the standard theory being touted at Ames that the "prettiest" ears of corn were the best producers. The results of the test, which were eventually published in *Wallaces' Farmer,* showed that symmetry, size, and fullness of ears of corn could not be used as good indicators of production in subsequent generations.

In 1906, Henry A. entered the animal-husbandry program at Iowa State College. He continued to be a serious student, receiving as his lowest grade an 87 in a course in animal judging, a subject he esteemed as little as the corn-judging contests that had prompted his corn-yield experiment. During his college career and later, when he was working at *Wallaces' Farmer* and assuming the family role as agricultural advocate, Wallace complained about the narrowness of the programs in agriculture that were offered at ISC. Students who wanted to pursue agricultural studies chose among five courses: agronomy, dairymaking, animal

[5] "Reminiscences," 28.

husbandry, horticulture, or science and agriculture. Although these programs had similar requirements for the freshman year, subsequent course work focused narrowly on the subject of specialization. Animal husbandry, the course that Henry A. chose, emphasized judging, selecting, breeding, feeding, development, care, and management of domestic animals. By the summer of 1909, when he made his tour of the West, in addition to the required courses in animal husbandry, Wallace had taken elective courses in plant and animal embryology and agrostology.

Throughout his life Wallace was an untiring student of foreign languages, and he put his skills to use in his trip through the West. In high school he had taken two years of Latin and two years of German. During his freshman year at ISC he added Spanish, a language in which he later became fluent.[6]

Although he did not lack friends, Henry A. continued to be somewhat unconventional socially during his college years. He was a member of the Hawkeye Boarding Club, a group that later became Delta Tau Delta fraternity. At their fiftieth class reunion, several of the men who had been young Wallace's roommates recalled their memories of him:

He had an unruly shock of hair, his shoes were unshined, his clothes "short of pressing," and he sometimes forgot to shave. But we knew by his countenance and actions he was

[6] Henry A. Wallace's academic transcript from Iowa State College, 1906–1910, in Biographical Data file, Henry A. Wallace file/Alumni Affairs/Alumni and Former Students, Series 21/7/5, box no. 1, Special Collections, Parks Library, Iowa State University, Ames.

doing some deep thinking. . . . He was half a jump ahead of the instructors in some classes.

He was always coming up with what the boys called a "screwy" idea. Once he and three others existed for quite some time on oranges, to see if this kind of light diet improved our ability to study. Another time we lived on a milk diet. I don't remember what. . . . One day he sheepishly admitted the animal husbandry department had been experimenting with a new kind of feed and he had been eating it.

Henry usually dated for fraternity parties, but was not a "regular." He was always a good visitor, but the conversation was on a high level. . . . I recall one house party at which, for entertainment, Henry invited his lady guest to visit the college poultry farm. . . ."[7]

Wallace usually did not remain on campus on weekends but went home to Des Moines, for it was there that his strongest intellectual support was found. He read widely in addition to his required course materials and found his grandfather to be the person with whom he could have the most stimulating discussions about new ideas.[8] This weekly family contact also kept him in touch with what was going on in *Wallaces' Farmer.* After the series of articles about his western tour, for which he received a by-line, Henry A. earned extra money during his senior year by writing for the family journal as a staff writer, usually without by-line and at the current rate the editors were paying.[9]

[7] " 'Chip of the Old Block,' " page unnumbered.
[8] "Reminiscences," 58.
[9] " 'Chip of the Old Block,' " page unnumbered.

In spite of his unconventionalities, Henry did some things at college because he thought he "ought to," such as joining the Welch Literary Society, one of the ubiquitous college debating clubs.[10] During his senior year he was on the editorial staff of the *Iowa Agriculturalist,* a monthly publication of the college's Agricultural Club, and had charge of the topic of "general agriculture." Among several articles that Henry wrote for the journal during that year was one that appeared in October 1909, "Dr. V. P. Cook's Dry Farming System," which was based upon an interview he had conducted during his summer tour.

During the first decade of the twentieth century, dry farming had been a topic of much discussion in the pages of *Wallaces' Farmer.* Because the editors of the journal sought to provide their readers with scientific principles on which to base farming, they contended that the information in their journal was as applicable in the newly opened regions of the West where dry farming and irrigation were being practiced as in the humid climate of the Midwest. And, following the thinking of Theodore Roosevelt and Gifford Pinchot, the Wallaces were conservationists, believing agricultural land was a resource that needed wise management. To them, irrigation and dry farming both represented means of managing the semiarid lands of the West.

Again and again the editors of *Wallaces' Farmer* asserted that they were not opposed to dry farming, as some had accused, but that they wanted to inform their readers of the economic dangers it could involve and also of the promotional schemes of land speculators. In addition to

[10] "Reminiscences, 65.

their own articles and editorials about dry farming and the irrigation projects, the editors published reprints of bulletins from the western experiment stations and letters from readers that told of both their successes and failures in the West. It was through this kind of correspondence, as well as Uncle Henry's trip in 1908 with the Country Life Commission, that the Wallaces became acquainted with some of the people young Henry visited during his tour.

As he began his westward journey, then, Henry A. Wallace left Iowa with a good understanding of the agricultural theories and practices he might encounter. He believed in conservation and considered reclamation projects a feasible way to utilize land that otherwise would be unproductive. In addition, he had a mind open to new ideas and admired the farmer who was willing to undertake experiments. Always ready to engage in conversation about that subject nearest his heart, agriculture, he provided an eager audience for those farmers who were willing to share their experiences with him. The tour marked the beginning of Henry A. Wallace's career as a farm journalist, a stepping stone that ultimately led him to even greater national prominence than either his grandfather or father had achieved. In 1933 he assumed the office of secretary of agriculture, and in 1940 he was elected vice president of the United States.[11]

---

[11] A number of works have been written about other aspects of the life of Henry A. Wallace. See Russell Lord, *The Wallaces of Iowa* (Boston: Houghton Mifflin Company, 1947); Edward L. Schapsmeier and Frederick H. Schapsmeier, *Prophet in Politics: Henry A. Wallace and the War Years, 1940–1965* (Ames:

Introduction

Irrigation Agriculture

When twenty-one-year-old Henry A. Wallace started "On the Trail of the Corn Belt Farmer" in the summer of 1909, it was his intention to report on irrigation agriculture in the West. And all but two of the articles he prepared do just that. The other two report on his trip to the Texas Panhandle, including a brief stay at the Alamositas Ranch of the Matador Land and Cattle Company. Otherwise, from Garden City, Kansas, to the Pacific Coast and then back to Iowa, his articles discuss both public and private irrigation projects, as well as reflecting on dry farming, based on conversations and observations. Wallace made it a point to talk with farmers and their wives, townspeople, ranch hands, managers, realtors, and others everywhere he went. His articles report their views and thus provide an invaluable insight into the early years of irrigation agriculture in the western regions of the United States.

Since much of the western country is arid, its agriculture involves irrigation. Today over 85 percent of the nation's irrigated acreage occurs in the seventeen western states. Anywhere from 10 to 13 million acres of the most productive lands in the West would be yielding little of value in the absence of irrigation. Instead, more than half the value of the agricultural output comes from irrigated lands. In

Iowa State University Press, 1970); Karl M. Schmidt, *Henry A. Wallace: Quixotic Crusade, 1948* (Syracuse, N.Y.: Syracuse University Press, 1960); Norman D. Markowitz, *The Rise and Fall of the People's Century: Henry A. Wallace and American Liberalism, 1941–1948,* (New York: Free Press, 1973); and "Henry A. Wallace and Iowa Agriculture," *Annals of Iowa* 47 (Fall 1983): 87–231.

California, the nation's leading agricultural state, over 80 percent of the total value of the produce comes from irrigated lands. Federal projects and subsidies helped ensure this development through reliable flows of affordable water, while state laws provided the assurance of permanent water rights.[12]

In 1909, when Henry Wallace went west, this development was in its infancy, just getting underway. Thanks to the Reclamation Act signed by Theodore Roosevelt in 1902, relatively inexpensive water was becoming available to western farmers. The government would build the works and sell the water to homesteaders and landowners for enough to repay the estimated costs. The payments for the water were to be made in not more than ten annual installments, with the secretary of the interior determining when the first payment should be made. Once these ten payments were made, the works were turned over to the water users for operation at their expense, though they remained under public control unless Congress deemed otherwise.

Initial water users were allowed to use available water without charge, and they were also granted the rights to use similar amounts in perpetuity. The only costs for the user were those of capturing and conveying the water. The vast irrigation projects that were underway when Henry Wallace went west in 1909 came under the jurisdiction of the Reclamation Service in the Department of the Interior,

[12] Kenneth D. Frederick, "Irrigation under Stress," *Resources,* Spring 1988, no. 91. Data from a boxed insert on p. 2. *Resources* is a quarterly publication of Resources for the Future.

whose director, Frederick Haynes Newell, a civil engineer, previously had engaged in irrigation surveys while a member of the United States Geological Survey under John Wesley Powell.[13]

While irrigation in the United States can be traced back to the Hohokam Indians in the Southwest, who as early as 100 B.C. constructed canals to irrigate crops in Arizona's Salt River Valley, modern irrigation began in the post–Civil War years when settlers adopted and expanded Spanish-American techniques. Beginning in 1877, the federal government consciously stimulated irrigation first by private and state involvement and then by direct federal participation. The Desert Land Act of 1877 and the Carey Act of 1894 accomplished the first two objectives. The Reclamation Act of 1902 achieved the latter. The 1910 Census *Bulletin* described the following types of enterprises engaged in irrigation activities in the arid regions:

Commercial Enterprises, incorporated or otherwise, which supply water for compensation to parties who own no interest in the works. Persons obtaining water from such enterprises are usually required to pay for the right to receive water and to pay, in addition, annual charges based in some instances on the acreage irrigated and in others on the quantity of water received.

Individual and Partnership Enterprises, which belong to individual farmers, or to groups of farmers associated without formal organization. It is not always possible to distinguish between

[13] Kenneth D. Frederick, *Water for Western Agriculture* (Baltimore: published for Resources for the Future by the Johns Hopkins University Press, 1982), p. 2; *Reclamation Record,* November 1909, discusses all of the projects under construction.

partnership and cooperative enterprises; but as the difference is slight this is unimportant.

Cooperative Enterprises, which are controlled by the water users combined in some organized form of cooperation under state laws. The most common form of organization is the stock company, the stock of which is owned by the water users. In Arizona and New Mexico many of the cooperative enterprises are operated under laws regulating "community" ditches.

Irrigation Districts, which are public corporations established under state laws and empowered to issue bonds and levy and collect taxes for the purchase or construction of irrigation works.

Carey Act Enterprises, established under the Federal law of August 18, 1894, granting to each of the states in the arid region, 1,000,000 acres of land on condition that the state provide for its irrigation, and under amendments to that law granting additional areas to Idaho and Wyoming.

United States Indian Service Enterprises, established under various acts of Congress providing for the construction by that service of works for the irrigation of land in Indian reservations.

United States Reclamation Service Enterprises, established under the Federal law of June 17, 1902, providing for the construction of irrigation works with the receipts from the sale of public lands.[14]

[14] *Thirteenth Census of the United States: 1910 Bulletin—Irrigation: United States,* "Introduction." This bulletin is a reprint of chapter 14, pp. 421–32 of the abstract of the Thirteenth Census, a copy of which can be found in the Carl Hayden Papers, box 617, folder 6, Arizona Collection, Arizona State University;

When Wallace went west, the preliminary stage of examination and survey by the Reclamation Service for the selection of projects was virtually completed. Construction was well underway, and large areas were already irrigated; however, the settling of the various projects and the collecting from their residents the cost of the works had just started. Wallace thus was able to view and report on federal projects getting underway and on more established and prosperous private endeavors. He was able to suggest comparisons. His assessments, while realistic, were nevertheless optimistic about the prospects of irrigation agriculture.

Of the terms used in discussing irrigation, *acre-foot* is most common. It indicates the volume of water required to cover one acre to a depth of one foot, or 43,560 cubic feet. Reservoir water surplus came largely from streams or wells, less frequently from collecting storm water or from ordinarily dry water courses. Other terms used by settlers on projects and elsewhere in the arid West as they sought to store the floods, reclaim the deserts, and make homes on the land, were precisely defined by Henry Wallace in preparing his reports.

The census data for the arid region as a whole, which

---

hereafter cited as *Irrigation Bulletin: 1910*. The description indented in the text is quoted verbatim in reverse order from the *Census Bulletin*.

Under the terms of the Desert Land Act a person could enter and secure title to 640 acres of land. Within three years the entryman was required to pay $1.25 an acre, or $800.00 and put water, costing about $10.00 an acre, upon the land. The majority of the land secured under this act was not developed by farm families, most of whom could not finance a small reservoir or a diversion dam upon the land.

according to the statisticians who prepared them was somewhat overstated, indicated a marked increase over the 1900 census in most categories. In 1910 there were 1,440,882 farms in the arid regions comprising the western parts of the tier of states formed by the Dakotas, Nebraska, Kansas, Oklahoma, and Texas and all of the area between them and the Pacific Ocean. This figure represented an increase of 345,147 farms since the previous census. Of these farms, 158,713 were under irrigation, compared to the 107,489 farms cited in the 1900 census. Most dramatic was the cost of irrigation enterprises owing to the thirty Reclamation Service projects under construction. The 1910 figure of $307,866,309 contrasts sharply with the 1900 figure of $66,962,275, an increase of 359.8 percent. In all, about 14,000,000 acres of irrigated land, about 80 percent more than had existed ten years previously, was noted in the 1910 census. Most of this acreage was provided by private enterprise with some aid from state and national legislation. Only about 1,000,000 acres came into production on Reclamation Service projects. In time, of course, these acreage figures would change drastically.[15]

What the figures do indicate is that the American people were optimistic regarding irrigation farming. Newly irrigated lands were attracting settlers seeking to keep pace

[15] *Irrigation Bulletin: 1910,* p. 422. Carl Hayden noted that up to June 30, 1913, 28 projects had cost $78,754,526.24. The total area that would come under irrigation when the projects were completed, he estimated, would be 2,973,048 acres on 60,569 farms. Crop returns on this acreage in 1912 was about $4,500,000. Total construction charges paid came to $3,241,275 as of the above date. See "Notes On Irrigation Bill" [1914], Carl Hayden Papers, box 617, folder 3.

with the projects under construction. Though very little irrigated land was available for homestead entry, considerable amounts of land in private ownership, if subdivided into smaller units, could have been farmed more suitably under irrigation. The estimate of 14,000,000 acres, the total of irrigated land in 1910, added up to little more than one-third the size of Henry Wallace's home state of Iowa. But, as Wallace noted in his reports, figures alone did not do justice to the real significance of irrigation agriculture. Its sole purpose was not to produce foodstuffs for eastern and European markets; irrigation agriculture also served to provide homes and develop a community outlook. It supported people engaged in stock raising, mining, and other endeavors in the West. In fact, in most of the areas Wallace visited, the products of irrigation were largely consumed in local or nearby markets, where, because they were far from producing centers in the Midwest and the East, they usually brought good prices. As production under irrigation agriculture increased and exceeded local demands, the surplus would come into competition with the products of nonirrigated lands. But Wallace did not believe that time had arrived; most irrigation communities had not reached that stage of development. And in the case of those that did, the California citrus growers, competition was not a serious factor. In 1909 modern irrigation development was still too new to yield clear indications as to what difficulties might be expected in the future.

What Henry Wallace saw was a brighter future for irrigation farmers based on intensive farming with a small acreage for individual families. This would lead to prosperous communities with better-developed infrastructures of roads, schools, and social institutions than prevailed in most rural regions. Moreover, irrigation crops need not compete with those produced elsewhere; rather they could complement the American diet, find a possible overseas market, and above all help sustain a growing population in the West.[16]

The original Reclamation Act, approved by Congress in June 1902, set aside the receipts from the sales of public lands in the arid western states as a reclamation fund. It was estimated that this fund would reach within a decade a sum of about $30 million. Moreover, the law provided that the cost of each project should be repaid to the fund by the settlers in ten annual installments. Thus renewed, the fund would be used in the construction of additional projects, thereby limiting the liability of the Federal Treasury and guiding the Reclamation Service in proposing new projects or adding to the cost of others.

The costs proved difficult to estimate as the Reclamation Service, in providing for distributing ditches, laterals, and power-development, pumping, and other supplemental features, engaged in cost overruns that, while Henry Wallace did not contemplate them, soon became a matter of congressional concern. Wallace was aware, however, of another matter that engaged public discussion, namely, that speculators held land included in irrigation projects along with actual settlers. Wallace also recognized that since

[16] Carl S. Scofield, "The Problems of an Irrigation Farmer," in the 1909 *Yearbook Of The United States Department of Agriculture,* pp. 197–208, and "The Present Outlook for Irrigation Farming," in the 1911 *Yearbook,* pp. 371–82, presents a cautious assessment befitting his position as the specialist in charge of the Western Agricultural Extension in the Bureau of Plant Industry.

much of the land included in a project might not be under cultivation, it would take a settler some years to clear, level, and plow the land before getting it under cultivation. While settlers were improving their farms and helping to develop communities on their projects, two or three years might pass before a cash crop could be produced.

With regard to the area to be held by homestead entrymen on irrigation projects, the 1902 law fixed the acreage between 40 and 160 acres, and the secretary of the interior, or his representative, a Reclamation Service official, suggested the size of the tract considered necessary for the support of a family on the lands. For those lands in private ownership, the law provided that no right to the use of water could be sold to any one landowner for a tract exceeding 160 acres. At the secretary's discretion water rights for less than this amount could be furnished to lands in private ownership, as was the case on public lands.

Heated controversy would erupt about the effectiveness of the Reclamation Act, whether projects were able to meet their payments, whether the Reclamation Service could compete on a cost-effective basis with private irrigation, whether the act needed serious modification, or whether it was merely maladministered. Another contentious issue was that water could be wasted and made useless for federal projects by private enterprises, especially when they were located far from the tracts the government desired to utilize for the construction of storage facilities. These and other related matters quickly engaged the attention of Congress, which in the early years of Woodrow Wilson's administration proposed legislation extending the time of payment to water users. However, none of these matters concerned Henry Wallace. His articles reflected markedly different concerns and were directed to a specific set of readers, corn-belt farmers and others in the Midwest who subscribed to *Wallaces' Farmer*.

What makes Wallace's articles both interesting and historically important is that they represent socially informed reporting, presenting individuals' responses to the transformation they were witnessing or had recently experienced as they adjusted to a new way of life predicated on irrigation or dry farming, or as in Wallace's articles on Texas, to life on the high plains. By seeking individual responses to life in the arid regions, Wallace illuminated a cultural response, life-styles markedly different from that of corn-belt farmers. The change involved a collective experience to meet social and economic needs related to irrigation agriculture. It demanded new initiatives as farmers met new challenges.

Situations affecting prairie farmers were not replicated in arid regions "under the ditch." Not only were the crops different, the way of life or the culture was also different. The combination of circumstances created by intensive farming brought individuals closer together into social and business relations that stressed cooperation more than competition. While the Reclamation Act set a limit of 160 acres upon any one farm desiring water, as Wallace and others observed, an operation of that size was exceptional. Even eighty acres under irrigation was considered a large tract for a family. Experience showed that forty and eighty acre units were in many instances too large for a farmer of moderate means. The great majority ranged in size from ten to forty acres.

Irrigation agriculture, publicly or privately developed,

on acreages up to forty acres properly attended, could provide comfort and independence, Wallace claimed, to any family. The limited acreages fostered economic cooperation by placing close together hundreds of farmers with mutual interests such as the allocation and economical use of water and the marketing of crops. Other forms of cooperation quickly followed. It was easy, for example, for an entire neighborhood to gather quickly in a school, church, or meeting hall, and yet not be out of sight of the residents' homes, which boasted shade trees and verdant lawns in the older developments. Irrigation farmers, as Wallace noted in a final essay, were social beings in a broad sense, as well as intelligent and alert businesspeople. They could not afford to be either loners or laggards. Pride and self-interest necessitated a communal life-style that produced, after a period of hardship, better and larger crops as well as greater profits through common shipments to market centers. Irrigation farming in 1909 offered attractive prospects for intelligent and industrious farmers. More could be achieved on less land, if it were under the ditch, than on farms elsewhere in the United States. Irrigation agriculture projected a vision of profit, leisure, and social intercourse that Wallace portrayed as within the grasp of any intelligent and hard-working farmer.

At the same time Wallace was aware of the speculators who acquired large areas of desert land that were valueless until water was available for their irrigation. Once this occurred, they could turn a handsome profit in selling off their acreage. These lands quickly became worth as much as those lands already being irrigated. Much of the money expended for laterals and head gates was raised by charging farmers excessive rates for water. However, while Wallace reported on the role of speculators, the problem was an emerging one and still largely theoretical. He did not pass judgment, rather he attempted to provide his readers with both sides of the issue through conversations with actively concerned individuals.

What Wallace indicates in these articles is that in the arid regions of the West farmers and ranchers, their families and others, experienced work, culture, and a collective consciousness in different ways than did corn-belt farmers and people in the regions with greater rainfall. Walter Prescott Webb two decades later would note a cultural fault line at the ninety-eighth meridian delineating this difference. Wallace in reporting conversations suggests how people in the region, particularly those in irrigated areas, viewed their world and how they related to one another in their trade, in their families, and in their communities.

A common experience that was collective rather than individualistic guided irrigation farmers as they sought to meet their economic and social needs. Outlines of the social structure, class composition, and family economy of irrigation communities are evident in Wallace's reports as he shows how a new environment and a new set of conditions called for adaptations that not all settlers could accept. Like a good reporter, Wallace placed people at center stage. He made it a point to talk with farm women to gain their perspectives. His articles brought men and women on irrigation projects to the forefront. In doing so he informed his readers about a new and significant development in its formative years. He was exposing what social historians today are greatly interested in analyzing, the culture of ordinary men, women, and children, seeing historical change from their perspective and not from that of elite leaders. Then, in his final three reports prepared in 1910 after he had returned to Iowa, he developed his overall evaluation of various aspects of irrigation agriculture.

Wallace presented an account that readers nine decades later will still find of consuming interest and great value. That they were written by a twenty-one-year-old undergraduate, albeit a remarkable one who was a member of an equally remarkable Iowa family, does not detract from his accomplishment. The articles in a real sense mark the first notable accomplishment of Henry A. Wallace, one hitherto largely unknown to biographers and historians interested in agriculture and the twentieth-century West.

❧ I ❧

On the Trail of the Corn Belt Farmer

The corn belt farmers have been spreading over the entire western country during the past decade, and especially during the latter half of it. It is a second "winning of the west." In practically every farming section of every state from the Missouri river to the Pacific ocean you will find men from Iowa, Illinois, and other corn belt states. They are in the dry farming sections and on the irrigated lands, in the grain country and in the fruit country, and in fewer numbers in the cattle country. With the purpose of giving readers of *Wallaces' Farmer* some idea of western agricultural conditions, and more particularly with reference to the irrigated districts, the writer is making a tour of the principal irrigation projects west through Kansas, New Mexico, Arizona, and southern California, up to Washington, and back through Idaho, Wyoming, Colorado, and Nebraska.

Garden City, Kansas

On this southern route Garden City, Kansas, is the extreme eastern point of irrigation. Garden City is a live town— the liveliest in western Kansas. They claim to have 400 miles of irrigation ditches in that neighborhood and 200,000 acres

Note: Chapter 1, "On the Trail of the Corn Belt Farmer," was published in *Wallaces' Farmer,* July 2, 1909.

of irrigable land; 40,000 acres growing sugar beets and alfalfa; a 90,000-acre forest reserve; a $1,250,000 sugar beet factory; they also claim to be the largest alfalfa and alfalfa seed shipping point in the world. There are about 4,000 people at Garden City, and they have the public improvements of considerably larger cities in the corn belt—telephones, electric lights, water system, sewers, cement sidewalks, etc. There are four different methods of irrigation in the Garden City district. First, irrigation direct from the Arkansas river; second, irrigation from reservoirs filled when the river is at the flood tide; third, irrigation by pumping from the underflow at a large central station; fourth, individual pumping plants, either by windmills or gasoline engines.

The first system, taking water direct from the river, is not dependable, for the reason that when the water is needed most there is none in the river, it having been all taken out by the Colorado people above. The reservoir system is used by the United States Sugar and Land Company above Garden City about sixteen miles. Here they have constructed a huge reservoir holding two and one-half million feet of water. It is a lake five miles long and two miles wide, and it is claimed has an average depth of thirty-seven and one-half feet. It is filled from the Arkansas river during the flood period. The third system is a government project. In the neighborhood of Deerfield, about sixteen miles above Garden City, the government has put in about $350,000 in establishing a pumping plant equipped with powerful turbine engines which furnish power to pump from something like 230 wells, tapping the underflow of the river. By this system about 50,000 gallons of water

27

can be pumped per minute. The estimate of the engineers indicates that by paying $3.50 a year for ten years the owners of the land under this ditch would pay out on the plant, take it over from the government, and own it themselves. So far the cost has exceeded this estimate. The United States Sugar and Land Company has a somewhat similar plant installed on the other side of the river. The fourth system mentioned, that of private pumping plants, seems to be very satisfactory. In some cases, windmills are used, but the more reliable power is the gasoline engine of ten to twenty horse power. With an outfit of this kind from twenty-five to seventy-five acres of land can be irrigated, the water being pumped into reservoirs and ditched from these as needed.

A fruit and truck farm in the suburbs of Garden City, "transformed from a bare spot by water from a well costing, with complete pumping equipment installed, $293" (from a photograph in the Eighteenth Annual Report, Kansas State Board of Agriculture, *1911–12).*

On the Trail of the Corn Belt Farmer

Among the farmers I interviewed was one from Illinois, said to be one of the best farmers in the district. He had a neat house surrounded by trees and 160 acres all under the government ditch. In reply to my questions he said:

"I have 160 acres in this place; 120 in alfalfa, no sugar beets. I raised some beets last year, getting a yield of sixteen tons to the acre. The factory paid $5 a ton. I netted about $20 an acre. Why don't I still raise beets? Well, I'll tell you. For one thing I have to bring in outside help—Mexicans, Japs, Russians, etc. Another reason is that the company has too much to say. The company contracts for a certain number of acres of beets; then it tells me just when I must thin them, when to hoe, cultivate, when to put on the water, when to top them, and when to deliver to the company's chutes. I don't like to be bossed in this way. Besides, I can make just as good money from alfalfa and get along without the outside help. I can farm this quarter almost altogether by myself. Last year I had great luck. My fields gave four and five tons to the acre. I sold this to the Sugar Company at $10 a ton in the field. There was not very much roughness here last year and alfalfa brought a good price."

I asked him what he raised in addition to his alfalfa. He said:

"I have been raising some Kaffir corn. I sowed it broadcast and sold it to the beet company at $7 a ton. Prices will not be as good this year, but I will get $8 a ton for my alfalfa in the field and $5 for the Kaffir corn. Water was very scarce last year; we had very little rain. The usual rainfall here is in the neighborhood of twenty-one inches. Last year we had less than a fourth of this."

I stayed to dinner with this man. His wife had a good dinner of bread, jam, potatoes, milk, beans, etc. It was very clear that she was a worthy helpmate, but it was not difficult to see that she was not as enthusiastic over the country as her husband. He was making money out of alfalfa, but she was lonely. She spoke of the continual blowing of the wind which made things seem all the lonelier. She and her husband both lamented the lack of people in the country. "There ought to be a family to every eighty acres at least," said the wife. "Now there are families only to the quarter sections, and they are so busy they never have time to see each other."

After dinner my friend went outside to sharpen the sickles of his mowing machine. He had an eight-foot mower of which he was very proud. The buck rakes were hauled in for repairs, and he was getting everything ready to go into the first crop of alfalfa, which he expected to do in a couple of days. He held his land at $100 an acre. Six years ago he bought it at $23 an acre. The previous owner had homesteaded it.

I left this farm and passed by several rather weedy beet fields. In one of them I saw some Mexicans at work thinning, and spoke to one of them in a mixture of English and Spanish.

"Buenos dias," I said, "cuantos pesos for one acre?" "Six dollars and fifty cents," he said. He told me there were some 300 Mexicans working around Garden City. A little later I saw a family of Germans at work in another field. There was the father, a big, hearty mother, two boys and two girls all hard at work on hands and knees thinning. With my German and the children's English I managed to make out that the family was thinning for $6.50 an acre and was making about $10 a day. The girls had overalls over their dresses. When I started to take the picture of the family working the girls immediately pulled off their overalls, greatly to the amusement of the mother.

The labor problem in the beet fields is a big one. The beets must be thinned, hoed, and topped by hand, and the total cost of the hand labor is in the neighborhood of $20 an acre. This work is done by Japanese, Russians, Mexicans and Germans, under contract. This system is liable to bring about slip-shod work on the part of the laborers. They know that the more beets they hoe out in the thinning the fewer they will have to care for later in the hoeing and topping, and unless they are watched carefully they destroy a great many. The beet cultivator is a special tool which cultivates four rows at once. Two disks are used to keep the dirt from the beets while between the rows is a single cultivator shovel. The beets are cultivated with this implement five or six times.

I interviewed a couple of young men who are "baching it" on 160 acres, all in alfalfa. For irrigation they were depending on the government ditch and seemed very well satisfied with the service they are getting from it, although the expenses have been running higher than they had expected, and there is some complaint on this account. Their view with regard to growing beets coincided with those of the Illinois farmer. They are selling their alfalfa to the beet company and expect this year to get $8 or $10 a ton for it in the field. They thought it paid them better to grow alfalfa than beets. These young men came from eastern Kansas and said they were going back there when the opportunity presented itself. They think irrigation is too expensive and takes too much time and work.

The farmers in this district are divided into two classes, the alfalfa growers, and the beet growers. The last two years have been poor beet years, being too dry in the early part of the season. The acreage this season, however, has increased to 12,000 acres, but this increase, as nearly as I could learn, has been due to the new men who have come in. The older farmers in that section are not enthusiastic over beets.

Down in the valley of the Arkansas river there is some splendid land, worth easily $150 an acre. The deep water underlies all of this lower land and splendid crops of alfalfa can be grown without irrigation, although they say it pays to irrigate it for hay. It is on this land that most of the alfalfa seed is grown, Garden City being the greatest alfalfa seed shipping point not only in the United States but in the world. After reaching the valley I stopped at a little place surrounded with nice trees. The owner of the place was stemming gooseberries with his wife and wearing one of her aprons. He was an Illinois farmer, and in reply to my inquiries concerning his alfalfa seed business he said:

"I do not irrigate any of my alfalfa. I have 160 acres of it which never was irrigated. I cut the first crop for hay; the next crop I allow to go to seed. It ripens along the latter part of August. This I cut with a self-rake set to bunch it. Then we buck it up to the threshing machine. Our expense is the cutting and threshing. Occasionally a third crop comes on fast enough to go to seed, and this is handled in the same way. I sell the straw for $6 to $12 a ton and the seed for $9 to $11 a bushel. Last year I got an average of $60 from each acre of alfalfa." From what I could learn as to the expenses connected with this I estimate that 75 per cent of this amount was clear profit. This man was very proud of his alfalfa seed growing operations and had won some premiums at Albuquerque.

The sugar beet factory of the United States Sugar and Land Company is one of the largest and best equipped in the Arkansas valley. It was erected at a cost of $1,250,000. The company fosters the beet growing industry with great care. It sells the best seed to the farmers, gives expert advice as to cultivation, watering, etc., instructs the farmer when to top, and directs him when to haul his beets to the factory. Early in the season the company contracts for so many acres. This year they have 12,000 acres under contract. They pay $5 a ton for the beets delivered at the factory when wanted. As before indicated, many farmers who last year and the year before grew beets are not growing them this year. Last season was an unfavorable one. There was not enough rain in the spring when the beets especially need it. The total expense of growing an acre of beets runs from $30 to $40 and the yield is from twelve to eighteen tons, for which the company pays $5 a ton. After a few years of beets the land must be put back to alfalfa. As more farmers come in and the farms are subdivided the beet acreage will no doubt increase. At the present time alfalfa is regarded as more satisfactory by the quarter section farmer. The hay is nearly all sold at home for good prices.

In the immediate vicinity of Garden City the live stock business is rather limited. On the dry upland back from the valley some very good cattle are grown and many of them are brought into the valley in the winter for feeding. From 1,500 to 2,500 head are fed on beet pulp and alfalfa at the sugar factory. Dairying would be very profitable in the valley, but so far no more milk and butter is produced than is needed for home consumption.

To the east of Garden City is a dry farming district. This section looks very desolate to an Iowa man. The Campbell system of dry farming is followed, and I saw a few good fields of wheat. The straw was very short but the stand was even, and the heads were there. This land sells for $10 to $15 per acre, depending upon the distance from Garden City.

The Texas Panhandle

I traversed the Texas Panhandle plains from end to end, from north to south, from east to west. I traveled by railroad, by automobile, by team and buggy, on horseback, and even on foot. I talked with all classes of men from many different sections of the country. I have not learned all about the Panhandle. It is a big country, two-thirds as large as Iowa, and no one in a short space of time can learn all about it. I have, however, learned something about it.

The Panhandle is one vast upland plain or plateau, broken only by the "breaks" of the Canadian, Red, and Brazos rivers. The "breaks" is a term given to the rough rolling country around the rivers, being too rough to farm. North of the Canadian river breaks the country is called the North Plain; south of the river are the Central and South Plains. The North Plains are rolling and dry. It is a cattle country, and probably will be for a long time to come. The Central and South Plains country is very level. There is not much variation either in the rainfall, soil, or crops grown. The difference in land values is mainly due to the distance from a railroad.

I came into the Panhandle over the Northern Plains country. The land is rough and rolling; the altitude is high,

Note: Chapter 2, "The Texas Panhandle," was published in *Wallaces' Farmer,* July 9, 1909.

and the rainfall scanty. In some of the draws and little valleys in the breaks there are some crops grown, but nearly the entire Northern Plain country is a cattle country. The big ranches still have a stronghold here. I spent a few days on the Matador Ranch, of which Murdo MacKenzie, well known to readers of *Wallaces' Farmer,* is manager, and in a future issue will tell something of the work on this ranch. The country is fenced into large pastures, some of them containing 100,000 acres. The cowman reigns supreme. The days of roping and rounding up the cattle are still in force. Readers of *Wallaces' Farmer,* however, are more interested in the Central and South Plains country, the farming country of the Panhandle.

My starting point for the Central and South Plains country was Amarillo, the metropolis of the Panhandle, and the chief trading point for all that country. Five years ago Amarillo had 1,200 people; now the population is estimated at about 14,000. It is a thoroughly up-to-date town with cement sidewalks, paved streets, electric lights, a street car line, churches, schools, etc. It can hardly be said to be an attractive town. It is set in the midst of a flat plain and has grown so fast that it has an unfinished appearance. The old town of three years ago with its old ramshackle buildings is still strongly in evidence. There are many fine new buildings and some very nice residences. Amarillo is not a good place in which to stop. The hotel accommodations are not sufficient. Coming in after six o'clock in the evening, I found it difficult to get a room in a decent hotel. This, combined with the flatness of the town site, the lack of trees, and the overgrown appearance, tends to give the new-comer a bad impression. But Amarillo will improve in these respects. It is a live, hustling town, and is growing faster than most of the small cities of the United States.

The Panhandle is dry this year. That is perfectly evident to anyone who has eyes. Wherever I went people were talking of the need of rain; except for a rain the first week in June there has been practically none since last fall. Grass is scarce and the short, nutritious mesquit barely affords pasture. It has been a discouraging time to both cattlemen and farmers, and the impression on the new-comer is not favorable. As I came to know the country better, however, I came to know that things were not as bad as they appeared. I found many new-comers discouraged, but the older residents all seemed confident. Over half of the rainfall, according to the government records at Amarillo, comes during the growing months. From Bulletin N of the Weather Bureau of the United States Department of Agriculture, giving the periodic variation of rainfall in the arid regions, I take the following average monthly and annual precipitation at Amarillo: January, 0.61 of an inch; February, 0.4; March, 0.5; April, 2.11; May, 3.95; June, 3.06; July, 2.77; August, 2.9; September, 2.05; October, 2.16; November, 0.7; December, 0.84. Average yearly, 22.39 inches. These averages cover a period of observation of twenty-two to twenty-three years. It will be seen from this that there is very little precipitation during the winter, which means a favorable winter for stock. This year the rain started in June; before that much of the ground was too hard to plow. Little planting was done before the middle of June.

I went west from Amarillo on the Santa Fe eighteen

miles to Canon City. The latter is typical of all of the larger plains villages, a town of about 3,000 inhabitants, growing fast, and showing it by its rough and awkward appearance. The attention of the stranger is attracted at once by the large number of windmills. Every house seems to have its own windmill. They are wooden wheeled, as they seem to stand the high plains wind better than the steel wheeled. Canon City gets her name from the Palo Duro cañon, formed by a branch of the Red river. This cañon is a splendid relief to the everlasting plain. There are trees and a running stream. I interviewed a farmer near Canon City, who said:

"Kaffir corn and milo maize are the big crops of this country. They always make crops, no matter how bad the season. We can plant as late as the first of July. The average yield is a ton of grain to the acre and we have been getting around $15 a ton. Last year I got a yield of a ton and a half of Kaffir corn to the acre and got $17 a ton for it. That, however, was above the average."

I asked about the preparation of the soil for this crop. He said:

"On sod ground we turn the sod with a sod plow, then drill in the Kaffir along in June. There is nothing to do then but wait for the harvest. The first year all the work is sod plowing, drilling and harvesting. The second year the weeds start to coming and we cultivate two or three times. We never fail to make a crop of Kaffir corn or milo maize."

I asked about corn. "Well, sir," he said, "we don't claim to raise corn very well here. The nights are too cool." (The elevation is about 3,600 feet.) "Sometimes there are big crops of corn grown around here, but we don't claim to be a corn country. The average yield probably runs about twenty bushels."

I asked about alfalfa. He said: "We don't have enough moisture in the winter to grow good alfalfa on most of our land. On the shallow water land we grow right good alfalfa. A neighbor of mine over here has some alfalfa land in a little valley which he holds at $80 to $100 an acre."

This farmer has been in the plains country for nineteen years. He has great confidence in the country. Near town he holds his land at $60 to $80 an acre; out further it ranges from $20 to $30 an acre. I talked with several other farmers near Canon City who gave me about the same idea as the one I have quoted. Milo maize and Kaffir corn are the staple crops. They do not know much about anything else.

From Canon City I went down through the heart of the South Plains. Ninety per cent of the country seems to be still in the unbroken prairie sod of mesquit. For miles and miles this would be the only thing to see. Dotted here and there several miles apart I could see windmills, the signs of habitation. Occasionally we would pass some broken ground, a very small amount of which was planted, or at least if planted the crop had not started. I saw some fields of Kaffir corn about six inches high that looked well. There were a few fields of wheat and oats; the stand was very even in most cases, but the outlook for a crop was not encouraging. The straw was very short and many heads were white. As I went south the country brightened; the altitude is less as you go south and they had evidently had more rainfall, due, however, to local rains. The grass had a greenish tinge and here and there I saw basins of standing water. These latter were from half an acre to an acre in size. There are no regular small streams in this section to carry off the water. It is either soaked up by the ground or collects in the basins and evaporates. I saw a nice field of Indian corn about eighteen inches high which had been cultivated once or twice and seemed to be absolutely clean. We passed one of Campbell's dry culture farms just outside of Plainview. The crops on it were looking fine; there was a beautiful stand of oats and wheat and a fair chance for a crop in spite of the dry weather; the corn and Kaffir corn looked well. Going into Plainview we passed through several future additions, indicated by a long series of white stakes. The real estate men of the town are anticipating its future growth. In the edge of the town is a large concrete building being erected for the newly established college.

On the train going down to Plainview I had formed the acquaintance of a very pleasant southern gentleman, a Mr. Bassett, who has been in the South Plains country twenty-six years. From him I acquired much valuable information. After supper we walked over Plainview together. I saw several splendid buildings, among them two fine concrete bank buildings, a reinforced concrete hotel in process of construction to cost about $75,000, and a number of very good business buildings. The people here are doing the wise thing in using concrete for their business buildings. Around the little court house are some nice young locust trees, almost the only trees in town. Everywhere were windmills and automobiles. The autos whizzed by in twos and threes, and Mr. Bassett told me that there were 150 cars in town. I saw some young girls driving merrily along at a twenty-mile clip. There are quite a number of nice driving horses in Plainview.

In the evening we sat on the front porch with six or seven other patrons of the hotel and talked about the country. Three of us were from Iowa, one from Pennsylvania, the others from southern Texas. For two hours we talked the possibilities of the Panhandle. The evening was cool with a delightful breeze from the south. Most of the talk was on land values. Land everywhere has increased tremendously in price in the past year. One of the Iowans had bought land in March, fairly close to a little town without a railroad. Now, four months later, his land had doubled in value. The town has grown to it. A southern Texan told me of a man (whom I afterwards met) who had bought land near a little town last year at $12.50 an acre and sold it this spring at $50. All the talk was optimistic. But only two of these men were farmers; the others were real estate men who were enjoying the rapid increase in land values. The farmers, however, were optimistic in spite of the present dry season. One of them spoke of a neighbor who had just sold his last year's oats at 60 cents a bushel and his wheat at $1.40. They were counting sure on a good crop of Kaffir corn. Not long after 9 o'clock the talk waxed slower; heads began to nod. This is the greatest country for sleep I ever saw. No one keeps late hours.

The next morning, in company with Mr. Bassett, I started further south across the plains by auto—a big six-cylinder car. The roads were perfect and we sailed across the country at from twenty to forty miles an hour—mile after mile over unbroken prairie. There were a few scattering houses and occasionally a fence. The land in this neighborhood south of Plainview runs about $15 an acre. Fifty miles from Plainview and from the railroad we reached Crosbyton, and five miles from this we reached Mr. Bassett's home, in a cañon formed by a branch of the Brazos river. He has a beautiful stone house, a never-failing stream running in front of it. The stream forms a series of beautiful falls and below the falls a splendid swimming pool. Here I enjoyed true southern hospitality, and it was with distinct regret that I left this beautiful home surrounded by trees, hills, and running water—such a contrast to the wide, flat plains.

At the little town of Crosbyton I talked with many people. All were optimistic of course. I talked with some of the women and found them not so optimistic as the men. "You like this country pretty well, do you Mrs. _____?" I asked of a tired looking little woman who had come with her husband from a northeastern state. She answered somewhat wearily, "Yes; it is awful healthy here, but it is mighty lonely. My daughter seems to mind it more than I do." Then her daughter spoke up: "There is nothing doing at all around here for the young folks," said she. Her mother continued: "In the spring the wind is frightful; the ground is dry and the wind blows across the plains for days at a stretch."

I took a drive over the country around Crosbyton. It looked exactly the same here as through the country to the north through which I had come. The soil is perhaps a trifle more sandy. Not much of the land has been opened up for farming. Nearly all that is broken was broken this year for the first time. They plow the sod about two inches deep, turning it completely over. They use a regular sod

42

plow with bars instead of a moldboard, making less draft and doing just as good work. I saw several pieces of this sod ground which had just been planted to Kaffir corn, practically the only crop grown in this neighborhood. Much plowing was yet in progress June 20th.

The traction engine is coming in. I saw one gasoline outfit at work pulling two gangs of big disks. The disks can be used when the ground is too dry for the moldboard plow. They do not do as good work as the moldboard but plow a little deeper. They do not turn the sod over so well. I watched this outfit at work. The engine moved right along at a two-and-a-half-mile-an-hour gait, cutting a ten-foot furrow of sod. They figure that an outfit of this sort will plow around thirty acres a day. The engine cost about $2,350 and the two gangs of disks around $800.

I ran across a 300-acre young orchard, probably the largest in the Panhandle. Cultivation has been good and the trees were in fine shape.

From Crosbyton I drove across to Emma, the county seat of Crosby county. This town has no railroad; in fact, there is none in the county. The striking thing about Emma—and this applies to all of these little non-railroad towns—is the large number of loafers in front of the little stores. Some of these men own several sections of land, but hire someone to do what is done there and spend their time in front of some grocery store in old overalls and slouch hats, expectorating tobacco juice vigorously and occasionally becoming energetic enough to tell stories. One slouchy individual whom I had seen at Crosbyton the day before had moved from the Crosbyton grocery store to the one at Emma. This fellow was the picture of dilapidation—

a frayed moustache, scattering chin whiskers, battered hat, and shiftlessness all over; yet he owned several sections of land and was reported to be quite wealthy. His son was at home working the land.

At Emma I met a young fellow who had fallen into the same shiftless habit, and whose chief accomplishment seemed to be prevarication. He told me of his father's farm some ten miles north, where he said they raised alfalfa seed at the rate of fifteen bushels to the acre, for which he got $15 a bushel. He also said his father had a fine orchard and that he was getting a yield of sixty bushels to the acre from his corn, etc., etc.

I drove over to the old man's place. He really did have a fine place. The orchard of peaches, pears, apples, and plums was in good shape. Last year it bore bountifully. This year a late frost caught all of the fruit. The farm showed marks of good care everywhere. The corn was as good as any I have seen, having been continuously cultivated and being entirely free from weeds. Like most of the corn here, it was drilled. This man did not have much to fear from dry weather, as he kept a beautiful dust mulch on all of his ground. The Kaffir corn was about four inches high and looking fine. He had a small field of cotton—the first I had seen in the range country. It was just up and receiving its first cultivation. For the past eight years this man has averaged half a bale of cotton to the acre. Cotton is an exacting crop, and as the plains are cool for it, very little is raised. There was a nice windbreak of locust trees on this farm. The old gentleman raised no alfalfa, notwithstanding his son's assertion, but is intending to plant some the coming spring.

West of Emma about thirty miles is a small town called Lubbock, the county seat of Lubbock county. It has a population of about 2,500, and is said to be the largest town in the United States without a railroad. There is, however, one in process of building, and Lubbock land values are soaring.

Most of these little towns have railroads in prospect. They are coming into the South Plains country from all directions. As the proximity to the railroads determine land values very largely in this country, the coming of the road is watched with tremendous interest. Many railroads are being built by local concerns, with the hope that they will be taken over by the larger systems.

Everywhere in this country the belief is firmly held that the rainfall is sufficient. Everyone seems to believe that when the country settles up there will be more rain. "Look at Kansas," they say. When I first saw the plains country it seemed to me a desolate place. It is more of a change than one first appreciates from the luxuriant vegetation of Iowa, Missouri, and Kansas to the short, dry grass which covers the plains of the Panhandle. There seems to be nothing to the country but one broad plain covered with this short grass. Of course at this season of the year the contrast is most marked. The real estate men of this country do not care to bring buyers down now; they wait until August or September. By that time the rains have come and the plains are a beautiful green; Kaffir corn has made a rank growth; the country has on its Sunday clothes. Much of the land is held by old cattlemen who bought it years ago for a song. They don't understand farming (perhaps they understand it as well as they want to) and are selling their land at a good price. During the selling season farmers from Iowa, Illinois, and other corn belt states are brought down by the car load and train load. They are met at the station with automobiles, whirled off into the country fifteen, twenty, or even fifty miles, and sold before they fairly get their bearings. Some of these men repent at leisure; the women folks get homesick; the dry season comes on; the wind blows; there are no trees. But after a season or two they become more contented, and finally firm believers in the country; that is, those who stay.

The soil, the climate, the crops, and the people of this country are all interesting. The soil is a sort of brownish red, or chocolate color, with a clay subsoil, and runs remarkably uniform. Toward the south it becomes more sandy. It works splendidly mellow and friable, much better than our corn belt soil in this respect. The surface soil is from one to three feet deep and is stored with the plant food of thousands of years of prairie grass. It yields abundantly when first plowed. How it will last no one can tell, as it has not been cultivated more than a few years. It is probably rather poor in nitrogen and humus, but nobody worries about that. The chief thought of the folks here is the rainfall. From the precipitation figures which I have already given it will be noticed that the large part of it comes during the growing season, and if it is well taken care of it should be sufficient to produce good crops. The older farmers here, however, are not informed concerning the principles of soil cultivation and the conservation of moisture. Few of them have ever heard of the Campbell system. They do not need to cultivate much to keep down weeds. The soil is so easily worked that any up-to-date farmer who is willing to work can save practically all of the moisture which falls and compels it to come up through the crops. There is great opportunity here for scientific methods of farming.

The climate is one of the points concerning which the true Panhandler boasts. The altitude ranges from 2,800 to 3,800 feet, and as a consequence the nights are cool and the breeze is always blowing. The days are very warm in the open, but at no time did I strike a day that seemed as warm, on an average, as our average Iowa June day. The cool nights make sleeping a delight.

Everywhere through the Central Plains country water is easily reached at a depth of sixty to two hundred feet, striking the sheet water here. This is pumped by means of windmills. Although the natives profess not to need irrigation, there is a great opportunity for using windmill irrigation in a small way to raise alfalfa and garden truck.

The crops of the plains country are Kaffir corn, milo maize, Indian corn, wheat, oats, and garden truck. Kaffir corn is the big crop. It seems to be always sure, and can be planted as late as the last of June. The yield runs around a ton to the acre; this sells for $10 to $17 per ton, or has been selling at these prices. As a feed it is much like Indian corn, but is worth only 85 to 90 per cent as much for fattening purposes. The nights are too cool for Indian corn to make a big crop. Those who grow it either drill or list on ground that has been broken several years. They secure from fifteen to twenty bushels to the acre; although I have learned of some yields of forty to fifty bushels to the acre when the seasons were very favorable. Wheat and oats make good crops when the spring is not too dry, but they are uncertain.

The plow has hardly made a mark in this country. Most of the land is in pasture. The grass is a short, nutritious mesquit, and it is claimed that in a favorable season seven to ten acres will support a cow. This was formerly a great buffalo and antelope country. This year the season has been very hard on the cattle, and in some places many are dying for lack of feed and water. This, however, is hurting the rancher rather than the farmer. The true Panhandle farmer does not handle much beef stuff, or, in fact, any live stock. His chief business is raising Kaffir corn and waiting for the land to increase in value. This of course will have to change if this country becomes an agriculture country. It is out of the question for the average farmer to make a permanent success here unless he handles live stock and makes that one of the main features of his farming. Dairying should be very profitable; there is one excellent dairy herd of forty Jerseys, some of which are producing twenty-five to thirty pounds of milk per day, and all of them are doing well. Good hogs can be raised on Kaffir corn. Chickens and all kinds of poultry do well. There is no dampness to kill off the young chickens. There is a great field here for horse breeding. At present there are a few good horses, and most of these are of the roadster type. Some good mules are being raised.

The people in the South Plains country are all very hospitable. They are a high type morally. There are no saloons in the Texas Panhandle. The Sabbath laws are very strict; I found, for instance, that ice cream can be bought on the Sabbath, but not ice cream soda nor oranges. Rules against gambling are strict. There is no card playing in this country. A game with dominoes called "forty-two" is played in the hotels. Nowhere except in Amarillo did I see a negro.

It is evident that there is a future for the Panhandle. With the influx of farmers from the corn belt good farming methods will be introduced; better crops will be grown; more live stock will be raised; more schools and churches will be established. Many who come will be discouraged. Each one must make up his mind to suffer the inconveniences of the pioneer, the lack of social intercourse, etc. This will be harder on the women folks than on the men. The corn belt farmer who comes into this country should own at least a section, and the more the better. Those who handle a large amount of land should operate with traction plows. The man who expects to buy in this country should come down here as soon as possible and see it before the summer rains change its appearance. The best time for the buyer to come is in April, May, or the early part of June. He then sees conditions at their worst. It is to the seller's advantage of course to bring him later in the season. Land prices have increased very rapidly during the past year; it has been a land boom. Folks who bought a year ago and have seen their land double in value are of course enthusiastic about the country.

❧ III ❧

The Salt River Valley

Going west and south from the Texas Panhandle through the deserts of New Mexico the land becomes flatter, the grass shorter and drier, and the country generally less inviting. Scattered along the road in plain sight of the train were many bodies of cows and steers dead from lack of pasture and water. There are more grade Herefords in this country than any other breed. They have a better reputation as rustlers than the Shorthorns.

I talked with some fellow travelers concerning this New Mexico land. Several had homesteaded in the dry sections. Of the four homesteaders to whom I talked three were Germans and one an American. These men had homesteads of 160 acres each. All of them mentioned the new act of congress which now permits the homesteading of 320 acres under the Desert Land Act. According to these men, Kaffir corn is the main crop on the dry lands of New Mexico. The government permits the homesteader to commute; that is, pay out on his land after having lived on it fourteen months. One of these homesteaders with whom I talked was intending to take advantage of this provision soon, paying $1.25 an acre for the land.

At one station, as the train went on through the desert,

Note: Chapter 3, "The Salt River Valley," was published in *Wallaces' Farmer,* July 23, 1909.

a bunch of Mexicans were taken on. They are largely used for railroad road work through this country. After a time a Mexican woman, well dressed, dropped into the smoker to smoke a cigarette. As we got into Arizona the scene changed; mountains appeared. Here and there we ran through a stretch of level plains covered with mesquite brush (not mesquit grass referred to in my letter from the Panhandle) and sage brush, with a little grass between. In these plains they evidently have severe sand storms. I saw huge drifts of sand quite frequently. As we got into the mountains pines and cedars began to appear, and after awhile we passed a saw mill. There is a big timber country to the north of the Santa Fe in Arizona—one of the largest forests in the United States. It is not like an eastern forest, however; there is no grass. Pines are scattered here and there among the barren rocks. North of Williams is the Grand Cañon of the Colorado, one of the most magnificent sights of this sort in the entire world. If any readers of *Wallaces' Farmer* go west by this route they will find it well worth their while to take this side trip from Williams up to the Grand Cañon, and if they want to become thoroughly imbued with the majesty and grandeur of the scenery take a walk from the top down to the river. A fourteen-mile trail winds back and forth down the sides of the cañon; while not dangerous, yet it is sufficiently awe-inspiring to trouble your sleep at night. The coloring is wonderful.

Phoenix, Arizona

Going down to Phoenix the Santa Fe slowly winds through the mountains and desolate desert valleys; at a few of the widely scattered stations there were evidences of small attempts at irrigation. But when we entered the Salt River valley the change was most marked. Here we found farm homes, trees, alfalfa, sugar beet fields—the first real agriculture in evidence in a trip of more than six hundred miles. Phoenix is a very pretty little city of about 20,000 population. No streets are paved or even oiled. The main streets are watered to keep down the thick dust, but the others wallow in a thick, yellowish-brown dust. The buildings are modern and fully equal to those of an Iowa town of the same size. The hotels are all provided with broad verandas, one above the other, for outdoor sleeping. Beautiful squares surround the public buildings. The grounds of the territorial capitol building are especially beautiful, filled as they are with many kinds of shrubs and beautiful flowers, dense headed Chinese umbrella trees, graceful pepper trees, long-leaved palms, oleanders, privets, pomegranate, orange trees, and ornamental bamboos, which are everywhere in evidence, and roses filled in between. The temperature at Phoenix reaches 100 nearly every summer day and frequently runs many degrees above that. No coats are worn. I went to church Sabbath without my coat. Electric fans were suspended from the ceiling of the church, while in the anteroom was ice water. From the pastor's announcement I found that services were to be suspended during the hot season, during July and August. After the sermon I heard some members congratulate the pastor on the brevity of the sermon. Sabbath evening the town was crowded; the squares overflowed with loungers. The Salvation Army was strongly in evidence. I sat in the public square and observed the people, at least five distinct types. There were many of our wide-awake hustling

52

Americans and alongside of these were the Mexicans talking away in their soft, throaty ways, a few Apaches with squat features and straight black hair, a number of Chinese and Japs, wide-awake and progressive, and our southern negroes, sleepy and easy-going.

Phoenix is the metropolis of the Salt River valley, one of the most wonderfully productive sections in the world. The soil is very fertile and the climate most favorable for vegetable growth. The valley is about forty miles long and the width varies from fifteen to thirty miles. It is evidently much like the California of fifteen years ago. Nearly every one in the valley seems to have come here for his health, or for the health of some member of the family. It is filled with "lungers," "t.b.'s," or "con's." Because of the dryness of the climate and the abundance of sunshine, conditions are most favorable for those suffering with tuberculosis. It is interesting to note that Phoenix has about the same latitude as Jerusalem, and I fancy that conditions here are very similar to the land of Palestine. Water has the same precious value as David places on it in his Psalms, while about Phoenix, as round about Jerusalem, "The mountains ever stand."

Monday morning I set out to see the farming country, devoting the forenoon to an automobile trip. Three miles north of town we passed the Indian school. The grounds are well kept, the buildings are of substantial brick, and everything is to the credit of the government. We passed many alfalfa fields, a number of them being used as pasture for dairy cows. Alfalfa is the main pasture here. It is used the year round and furnishes splendid pasture for all kinds of stock.

The alfalfa is irrigated by flooding between ridges. Fruits, vegetables, and corn are irrigated by the furrow system. The frequency of irrigation varies with the crop and the amount of water available. The alfalfa is irrigated once for each cutting, or every five or six weeks. Fruits are irrigated once or twice a month.

Going east, nearer the mountains is the orange belt. The mountains keep off the cold winds. This year the orange crop will be rather light, owing to early hot weather, followed by comparatively cool weather. The trees in the groves we passed were young, about eight years old, and rather small as yet, but were bearing fairly well. The groves are not kept in as perfect a state of cultivation as I had expected. There were but few weeds, but not the perfect

Irrigation in the Salt River valley near or in Phoenix, Arizona, circa 1908 (Salt River Project Archives)

An Indian (probably Pima) irrigating from a Reclamation Service canal near Sacaton, southeast of Phoenix, circa 1908 (Salt River Project Archives; photograph by Walter J. Lubken).

surface dust mulch which I had supposed would be necessary in a climate of this sort. In most cases the ground was hard and crusted from the last irrigation. We stopped at the orange grove of an Indiana man who came out to the country several years ago with no money, no health—nothing in fact, but some ambition. Now he is working forty acres of orange land. He had just planted some cowpeas between the rows. The soil is exceedingly rich in everything but nitrogen and humus. Orange trees must have plenty of nitrogen, and this was one reason for planting the cowpeas, to save buying nitrogen in the form of guano. Compared with the orange growers of California, the Salt river orange growers are tyros. As one man expressed it,

"The California man will tell you more in five minutes about orange trees than we can tell you in five hours." But these men claim to get results, and claim they can beat the California man at his own game even if they don't know much about the fine points of it as yet. All the Phoenix people will tell you that their oranges beat the California oranges to market. They are undoubtedly earlier, for they reach the New York market by Thanksgiving, while the California oranges do not get there until Christmas. As for quality, they claim that the Salt River valley oranges are sweeter because of the unusual amount of sunshine. Any advantage orange growing may have here over California is due to the fact that the season is a month earlier, the soil very fertile, and the extreme amount of sunshine which holds in check fungus diseases. What the orange growers of the Salt River valley seem to need is more knowledge of the business and a more thorough application of this knowledge. Under present conditions there seem to be large profits in orange growing here. They set eighty to ninety trees to the acre; these commence to bear at five years of age, and in two or three years more yield from two to four boxes to the tree. A box in New York sells for from five to nine dollars.

There is a large amount of expense connected with the growing of oranges, and a comparative estimate of net income from a seven or eight-year-old tree is $3.00 to $4.00, or around $300 an acre. Last year one man here made $7,000 net profit on twenty acres. The other side of the story is that to get improved land here that will grow oranges one must pay from $150 to $300 an acre, and then spend $600 to $800 an acre to get it covered with bearing trees. Then there has been some trouble securing sufficient water, but everyone here hopes that this trouble will disappear in 1910 with the coming of the government irrigation from the big Roosevelt dam. If this pans out as it is hoped, there will be a tremendous increase in the orange industry of this section in the next five years. An Iowa farmer would have to change his methods very radically to handle an orange grove successfully. Like all fruit business, it is puttering work and takes lots of care. Intense cultivation must be given. A great many city men in poor health are very successful in it and probably just as well adapted to the orange business as the average farmer.

Securing a bicycle, I took a long ride into the country. The roads are thick with yellow dust, but perfectly level. Near town they are lined with long, beautiful rows of palms on either side, while further out cottonwoods are used for this purpose. Along the roads were laterals of the main irrigating ditches. Some of them were running full of water; others were dry. Most of the land appeared to be in alfalfa. It is the big crop of the valley. Nearly half of the 200,000 acres here is in alfalfa and, as before stated, it is the main pasture and all the dairy cows which furnish milk in Phoenix are pastured on alfalfa the year round.

I stopped to talk with several dairymen and look over their cattle. The dairy stock I saw compares most favorably with the dairy cows of Iowa. I found representatives from all of our common beef and milk breeds and some very superior grades of the Short-horn type. The most common breed here, however, and evidently the coming breed, is the Holstein. The Holstein cow's capacity for a large amount of pasture and her large milk yield make her a favorite. I asked one dairyman how he handled his cows through the year. He said: "We pasture them the year around on alfalfa, and that is about all there is to it. We never feed any grain. In the winter we help out the pasture a bit with alfalfa hay. We have no barn or shelter of any kind for the cows. In November, December, and January we can drill barley in the alfalfa, and this helps out the winter pasture. In May the barley can be cut for hay, and the alfalfa disked and irrigated. Then it can be left for hay or pasture during the summer."

I asked the prices for his milk and cream. He said: "For the whole milk I get $1.20 a hundred pounds in the summer and $1.50 in the winter." Further out, he said, the dairymen were separating the cream and got 20 cents a pound for butter fat. His wife is an Iowa woman and I talked with her a little about the country. She said: "I like the country splendidly. I took the children back to Iowa last summer for a visit, but we were very glad to get back to the Salt River valley. But then I think I would be happy wherever my family is. Iowa is nice, but Arizona is nice, too. I came out here twelve years ago with my sick mother. It was a little lonesome at first, but since the first year I have liked it very well."

I rode on down the dusty road. In spots the dust was so deep that it was impossible to make progress with the bicycle. Some land along the road had evidently been in cultivation but abandoned and now [was] covered with a few mesquite bushes. I afterwards learned that this land had been brought under cultivation during a series of years when there was an abundance of water; then the diversion dam washed out with the flood and there came a series of dry years, making water scarce. The orange trees suffered severely, much of the alfalfa died, and a considerable amount of land went back to mesquite brush. Since the government has completed the diversion dam a ruling has been made that all land which has had no water for more than five years should go without water until the big dam at Roosevelt is completed.

Riding on I came to a rather deserted looking house. The land around was partly in alfalfa, but mostly in mesquite brush. I stopped to get a drink. The man told me to go over to the "olla" (oya) and help myself. I looked around and saw a rather large jar covered with gunnysack, hung up in the shade of a tree. This was my first experience with an olla, but not my last, for I soon began to look upon it in the same manner as the small city boy looks on the soda fountain. The principle of the olla is that evaporation makes the water cool. I drank long and deep at this first olla. The owner told me that the water came up from the well at a temperature of 73 degrees but cooled in the olla to 68 and less. This man had been two years at the Ohio State University. During vacation some nine years ago he had an opportunity to secure work as a helper on a dairy farm near Phoenix. He took the place, and has been in this valley ever since.

"Land don't look so very well here now, does it?" he asked. "Well, when the drouth came five or six years ago I managed to keep a part of it in alfalfa. The rest must wait until the dam is completed at Roosevelt. I think I can hang on to it another year or two. We thought we were to have water this year, but the accident at the tunnel fixed it so we will not get any government water before 1910."

I asked how he minded the heat. "Well, sir, it is not bad at all. The winters are fine; it never snows. It is simply a perpetual spring. The summers seem hot, but they are not so bad. You are here in the worst part of it, and the thermometer reads hot, 104 degrees quite often. It doesn't feel any hotter than 80 degrees back east; that is because of the evaporation. I have pitched hay in a temperature of 112 degrees, got up a good sweat, and then sat down in the shade, and really, you know, I got so cool I wanted to get up and go to work again. Evaporation does it. The value of the land here is going to be measured by the reading of the gauge at the Roosevelt dam."

I rode back to town along another road. Suddenly in a field on one side of the road, I noticed a large number of ostriches, strutting along with heads wobbling at every step. I stopped in to see the owner, who showed me over the farm. The birds are kept in long lanes of alfalfa. This is all they need to keep them, with the addition of hay in the winter. Some of them came up to the fence and looked at us in a very amusing fashion. Some pecked at the buttons on my shirt and at my watch fob. The owner took me to the incubator house and showed me a very interesting sight—one which he said not fifty people in the United States had seen—the hatching of an ostrich. I noticed a hole in one end of the egg, which the owner said he had picked there a few days before. He now broke off the shell and helped the young bird out, separated the umbilical cord and tied it so that the young bird would not bleed. It was about the size of a Leghorn hen. This man has 200 birds on eighty acres of alfalfa pasture. "The business," he said, "is extremely profitable, but there are difficult points in incubation which render it hazardous for the beginner." He told me that each bird yielded him about $30 a year for feathers. The birds live to be fifty to seventy-five years old. When four years old they start to breed, then a pair will reproduce itself about every year. A breeding pair is worth $600 to $800 and should produce $60 a year in feathers and $250 a year in additions to the flock. The expense consists mainly in incubation, taking care of the babies, and keeping the alfalfa pasture in good shape. This gentleman told me that three-fourths of the ostriches in the United States are in the Salt River valley. He was very hopeful concerning the industry, and thought that it would make probably the most important live stock industry in the valley. At present this industry represents the value of over $1,000,000.

The next day I rode west of Phoenix to the government experiment farm. Some sheep experiments are being carried on here, crossing the Tunis sheep on the Rambouillet. The results seem to be satisfactory. I saw some of the cross-breds. They were small and active with fleece much like the Merino but brown in color. The manager thinks the cross-breeds especially adapted to Arizona conditions on account of their greater activity. Nearly all Arizona sheep are of the fine wooled type. The two pests which bother sheep here are the bot fly of the nose and the head and the screw worm, the latter being one of the worst pests of the southern states. The adult, a fly, lays its eggs in barb wire cuts or other wounds and in natural openings on sheep, cattle, horses, and even man. The eggs hatch to a grub, which eats away tissue at a terrific rate. In man the eggs are laid in the nose, and death often results. It is, however, not common in man.

I had some talk with the fruit man at the government farm. He said that for oranges conditions were splendid, but that for peaches, apples, and pears the quality would be low. In his company I looked over the date orchard. The long, graceful fronds make a pretty sight. He told me that this orchard was of no value because the most of the palms were male. There are two kinds of palms and the fruit is borne by the female. As the males and females can not be distinguished until they bear, the chances of securing a profitable orchard are not certain. My impression of the government farm was that its work is not as strong as it could be made.

Further west is the sugar beet factory, a very large plant, and at this season running in full blast. The long sheds were full of beets. The manager of the beet growing experts who supervise the growing of the beets in the valley told me that they paid $4.75 a ton for beets. At present there are about 4,000 acres grown in the valley. The average yield per acre is ten to fourteen tons. The expenses of outside help, to thin, hoe and top, are about $17 an acre; seed, $3 an acre. An outside estimate for total expense would be about $30 an acre. The beets are planted during the winter, from December to March—the earlier the better. The factory here can handle eight times the amount it is getting at the present time. They have found it difficult to interest farmers in the beet business on account of the success of alfalfa and fruit, and the large amount of puttering work connected with the beets. I talked with one of the most successful of the beet growers. He was getting twenty-three tons to the acre, and he had in a quarter section; and as he summed it up, all there is to growing beets is to plant them early in good soil and give them good care. The best soil is alfalfa that has stood for a few years.

I stopped at a farm house and, after holding long and pleasant communion with the olla, gossiped a bit with the lady of the house. She chanced to be from Detroit, Michigan. I asked her how she liked the country. "Oh," she said, "I just hate it. If I could get away I wouldn't stay here if you would give me the whole town of Glendale. My husband brought me out here for my health, but I would rather go back to Detroit and die." She had been here only six months and was the only one whom I met who complained strongly about the country.

The next day in company with a real estate dealer I took an automobile trip to the south of Phoenix. We crossed the Salt river; there was just enough water in it to keep running. After a mile or so we got into the irrigated country. On either side were long stretches of alfalfa fields. I saw several bunches of steers grazing on the alfalfa pasture. These steers are brought down from the mountains, where they live mostly on the mesquite brush. At first they are very thin, but on alfalfa they soon pick up and after sixty days or so of nothing but alfalfa are shipped to Kansas City or California. We stopped at a 640-acre farm mostly in alfalfa, and in charge of an Iowa man. He told me how they managed their alfalfa. He said: "We get about four crops of hay a year, perhaps a seed crop, and then pasture for the winter. When we don't pasture we get six to ten tons

63

of hay to the acre, but nearly everyone here pastures. We cut later here than in Nebraska. We wait until nearly all the blooms are out. In November we usually drill in barley for winter pasture and cut the barley in June." This man had some land in small grain alone. He had irrigated thoroughly in October, plowed, irrigated, seeded, harrowed, and irrigated twice during the growing season. The grain was cut in early June. Now in July he will irrigate again and list to corn, which he will give three or four irrigations and cultivations. "Yes," he told me, "that is the beauty of this country. You can work out doors and grow crops all the year round; no more winters for me."

Alfalfa land here runs from $150 to $400 an acre, depending upon the closeness to Phoenix. Orange land runs much higher; $700 an acre with bearing trees. The soil seems to be formed by washings from the mountains and is very uniform. It resembles very much the yellow loess soil along the Missouri river in western Iowa. The variation of quality is mostly due to the amount of sand it contains. It is a fine soil to work and has very little alkali. The soil here contains about four times as much phosphorus as our ordinary Iowa soil, but runs very low in nitrogen and humus, containing probably not more than one-sixth as much nitrogen as the prairie soil of Iowa and Illinois. The alfalfa, however, builds up the nitrogen content, and after the soil has been in alfalfa a few years it will grow almost anything.

There is no land left for homesteading in this valley. All is under private ownership. When the big dam is finished at Roosevelt no man can get government water for more than 160 acres. This means that there can be little speculation. To get government water a man must own 160 acres and live on his land, and this will result in those who own large bodies of land cutting them up and selling them.

I took the train from Phoenix some twenty miles to Mesa, on the south side of the Salt river, a prosperous little town that is making a reputation for itself as a great canteloupe shipping point. The big crop, however, around Mesa, as everywhere else in this valley, is alfalfa. There is one large ranch of some 3,000 acres of alfalfa near town, all of it irrigated by pumping plants from wells. Irrigation by wells is increasing rapidly in this vicinity. The water is reached at from sixty to 200 feet. The government is putting down many wells which are to be pumped by electricity furnished by the power plant at the Roosevelt dam. The night I spent at Mesa was very hot, and during a large part of it sleep was impossible. At the 5:30 breakfast I mentioned the heat to an old-timer. He agreed that the previous night was hot, and then mentioned a certain July 3d, two years ago, when the thermometer stood at 117. He said no one slept that night. At 6 o'clock in the morning the stage for Roosevelt drove up. Roosevelt is sixty miles from Mesa and seventy miles from Phoenix. It is at this point that the government is building a tremendous dam across the Salt river that is to make a storage reservoir to irrigate the valley sixty miles away. In my next letter I will tell something about this dam.

The Big Dam at Roosevelt, Arizona

Roosevelt is in the midst of the mountains, forty miles from a railroad. From Phoenix it is reached by automobile, or by taking the train to Mesa and driving on by stage, as I did. The stage was quite like the one I had pictured in my mind—a heavily built vehicle drawn by four horses. I got the privilege of sitting beside the driver. For several miles we bowled quietly along over level roads and through a cultivated country. Then we reached the end of the irrigation and the scene immediately changed. The land was covered with mesquite brush and cacti. There were many tall giant cacti. The plain stretched away level to the mountains, everywhere so level that it is a tradition here than a long time ago this valley was inhabited by an ancient people prior to the Indians who leveled the ground and then irrigated it. The people of the valley point to certain indistinct mound-like openings to support this view. Within a few miles of the first relay the driver whipped his horses to a run; on reaching the relay station I climbed down and immediately interviewed the first olla in sight. No matter how much I drink here I get wonderfully thirsty in a short time. The horses changed, we started again. The road became rougher. We wound back and forth, in and

Note: Chapter 4, "The Big Dam at Roosevelt, Arizona," was published in *Wallaces' Farmer,* July 30, 1909.

out between the mountains. Then came the third relay. These horses would be balky, so the driver previously explained to me, and they were. Just after we passed a creek and were climbing a steep grade the roan balked and stopped the team. The driver used his long whip and a string of choice oaths, but to no effect. Then he climbed down, unhitched the roan, took a long, stout stick and gave him a thorough beating. Tiring of the stick, he resorted to the stake chain. The horse took the beating meekly enough but tried to strike a few times. After having administered what he thought was sufficient punishment, the driver hitched up again and we started off at a dead run. The roan was evidently so toughened by beating and so inherently "ornery" that he was none the worse for his experience. We passed several freighters. On most of the wagons there were five pairs of mules. From 2,000,000 to 3,000,000 pounds of freight are handled over this road monthly.

The scenery along the trail kept getting more and more striking. In spots it was similar to the Grand Cañon. The most beautiful spot was just before the Fish Creek relay. Here the road winds down the side of the cliff for two and a half miles. The government has done some wonderful work building this road. Much has been blasted out and much has been filled in. The construction cost the government $500,000, but the result is one of the best mountain roads in the country. As we wound down this road the driver pointed out the house at Fish Creek, 800 feet below us. Just before reaching Fish Creek we met a man hauling ground rock who stopped to pass the time of day with the driver. This man was highly wrought up. It seems that one

Roosevelt Dam, circa 1909 (Salt River Project Archives; photograph by Walter J. Lubken).

of the men on the road had threatened to thrash him on sight. For this reason he had got a permit from headquarters to wear a gun. "If George comes to thrash me," he said, "he will get a hole blowed through him; he kin lick me, I know he kin; but he ain't goin' to get no chance." His conversation along this line was plentifully garnished with oaths.

We drove on to Fish Creek for dinner. We ate lightly, for heavy eating is not conducive to comfortable riding in a stage coach. My driver proceeded to refresh himself in the bar room and told everyone he met about the man with the gun. As we started again I noticed he brought a bottle of whiskey with him. His tongue loosened a bit. Just as we got through tearing down a long hill at full gallop, sliding around corners on the edges of precipices and jolting from side to side over rocks he confided to me some of his joys.

"_____," he said, "I like to have a load of three or four women in behind and then get half drunk so I don't care, and then get the horses in a good strong gallop around the corners."

"Do they faint," I asked.

"No," he said, "but they sort of rend the air with their shrieks."

I didn't wonder. He told me many tales of his experience and personal prowess. Just before we got to Roosevelt a man stopped us and the driver delivered to him three bottles of whiskey. No whiskey is allowed in Roosevelt. Swinging around a corner on the side of the mountain, the big Roosevelt dam suddenly loomed into view. It was a magnificent sight. The Salt river flows in a cañon. On either side of the river rise high cliffs, from 500 to 600 feet. The dam is built across from cliff to cliff, stands straight up from the river bed some 150 feet, and will when completed stand about 100 feet higher. It looked as massive as the hills. Over one side was running a beautiful stream, making a fine waterfall. This is the only water the people of the Salt River valley are getting from the river this year. There is an immense amount of water backed up in the basin, but none of it is available this year. At the bottom of the dam is a large tunnel to draw off the storage water. Early this season the tunnel was open, but the pressure was too great and it was feared it would be destructive. Steel linings are to be put in the mouth of the tunnel, and when this is done it is hoped that all will be well. This will be done about the last of September. Until then not a particle of storage water can be used by the people of the valley. We drove past the dam and a beautiful mountain lake came to view, spread out with two great arms, one where the water had backed up the Salt river and the other where it had backed up the Tonto river. These two rivers meet just before the dam is reached. This lake, which will be the largest artificial lake in the world, is surely a gem in a wonderful setting. Rising from it on all sides are beautifully colored mountains, spreading away as far as eye can see.

We drove on two miles, past the dam, along the lake, to the new town of Roosevelt. There was an old town of Roosevelt, but it is now under the waters of the lake. It was situated on the bank of the Salt river, but as the dam rose the water backed up and the town was necessarily abandoned. The new town is built high and dry above the lake. It is a typical little western camp town, but there are no saloons. All provisions have to be freighted sixty miles. Under the circumstances the accommodations in the new town of Roosevelt are very good. That night I took a swim in the lake—a very delightful experience after the hot, dusty stage ride.

The next day I set out to see the dam in some of its details. It is the most wonderful piece of engineering which I have ever seen. When the government began work the first thing was to build the mountain road. The next to secure cement. To freight it over the mountain road would make the cost tremendous, so a cement mill was built, and cement is made from limestone and clay, both found in this vicinity. By manufacturing its own cement the government makes it at a cost of about $2.10 a barrel, or one-third what it would otherwise have cost. Then there must be power to lift the huge stones used in the dam, so a power canal was built at a cost of $1,000,000. Nineteen miles from the big dam a small dam was built to divert the water into the power canal. This is carried along at a gentle grade until it reaches the big dam, and here the water by its fall operates the turbine, making electricity which is used for power in operating the huge derrick, and provides electric lights as well, so the work can be carried on day and night. At one side of the dam is a quarry where men are engaged shaping the rock to be used. The average rock weighs about a ton and a half. After they are shaped up I saw them lifted by the electrically operated derrick and swung in position as needed on the dam, where they are cemented in place. The cement is carried to the dam in large carriers on overhead cables; 450 men are working here, some hired by the contractor and some by the government. A contractor is building the dam under the government inspection and with government help in many particulars. The dam is built into the rock of the mountain side, then thirty feet down into bed rock. When completed it will rise 280 feet above bed rock, or 250 feet above the surface. At the bottom its length is 200 feet and its width 170 feet. On top the length will be 1,100 feet and the width twenty feet. It will create a reservoir with an area of twenty-five and one-half square miles and a capacity of 1,284,000 acre-feet, enough water to cover 1,284,000 acres one foot in depth. At present the work is about two-thirds completed and it is expected to have it entirely completed sometime next spring.

Just below the dam is the power house. At present this is developing 2,000 horse power, but when all is completed it will develop around 10,000. Below the power house is the transmission house, from which runs the transmission line to Phoenix. In a short time Phoenix will be lighted by electricity from this source. The electricity will also be used by manufacturers. There are tremendous possibilities in the power side of the question, and the beauty of it is that all this power is developed without taking anything from the irrigation value of the water. It is a case of "keeping your cake and eating it too."

The cost of the dam will be nearly $4,000,000. The power developed at the power plant will partly be used to pump water in the shallow water district. About 50,000 acres will be irrigated in this way. When the government has its work completed the whole plant will be turned over to the people owning the land in the valley. These people will then pay for the plant in ten years, the amount being levied at so much an acre per year against all the land to be irrigated by the project. As the total cost will be around $6,000,000 and there are some 200,000 acres to be irrigated, it means that each acre must pay $3 a year for ten years, less whatever may be earned by the power plant. Besides this amount there will be a continuous expense for maintenance which will amount to from $1 to $3 an acre a year. This year the maintenance charge will average $1.65 an acre.

To secure the building of this dam by the government the people to be benefited were required to form themselves into an association known as the Water Users' Association. The land owned by the members of the association is security to the government. The government then advances the money without interest, using the funds acquired from the sale of public lands, and it is paid back by the users of the water who are benefited, and becomes a revolving fund to be used for still other projects.

After seeing the great dam I staged it back to Desert Wells, the last relay before Mesa. From Desert Wells I walked eight miles across the desert to the diversion dam at Granite Reef. The trip across the desert was very interesting. The vegetation was entirely different from anything we see in the corn belt. There were many cacti of different kinds, such as Saguara or Giant cactus, which looks like a green fluted telegraph pole, and the different kinds of smaller cacti and prickly pears. No grass was to be seen anywhere. Mesquite brush was scattered all over the plains. It looks like a bush locust tree and varies in height from one to ten feet. In this neighborhood it is about three to four feet high. Notwithstanding the desert conditions, there seems to be a great deal of small animal life. Little squirrels, floating a bushy tail upright behind them, ran across the trail. There are numerous lizards and rabbits, the latter resembling our cotton-tails somewhat, but smaller and browner. Once a jack rabbit jumped up like a scared calf and streaked across the plains. Occasionally I could hear a bird from the top of a Giant cactus. Being attracted by a peculiar weed at the side of a trail, I walked over to examine it, and found myself looking down upon a coiled rattlesnake about four feet from the weed. I tried to kill him with pebbles, but was not successful. The sun was setting and its rays struck with great force. I perspired very much, but did not notice it greatly on account of the dry air. I acquired a great thirst, however, and realized that I should have brought a canteen of water with me. I was very glad when

I sighted the camp at the diversion dam. The man in charge was very hospitable, but accommodations were not plentiful. For a bed I had a canvas cot in the open desert, and slept well.

The next morning I looked over the diversion dam. It is about thirty miles below the Roosevelt dam. The latter is to store up the flood water against the dry season, while the diversion dam is to divert the water to the irrigation canals—one on either side of the river. Many dams were placed at this point in former years for this purpose, but they were always washed out by the floods and then periods of drouth followed. Now all troubles of this sort are past and the valley is being served with more water than ever before, even though the storage water is not yet ready for use. This diversion dam was completed June 13, 1908. It is 1,100 feet long and runs from twenty to twenty-six feet high. On either side of the dam and just back of it are sets of huge headgates. When open these permit the river water to enter the canals, one on the north and the other on the south side. The north side canal irrigates the country around Phoenix and to the north, while the south side canal will irrigate the country around Mesa and Tempe.

I talked with one of the government employees who tends the gates and is supposed to be one of the wisest men on irrigation in the valley. I said to him: "I see this water here flowing from the river through the headgates into the canal; now that it is in the canal, how does it get on the land which it is to irrigate?"

"Well," said he, "this water goes down the main canal; off the main canal there are a large number of laterals. The water does not run down the laterals all the time, but just when the headgate to a lateral is open. Suppose, for example, there is a man who has forty acres of alfalfa he wants to irrigate. He is on a lateral with six other farmers. These seven men all work together. They appoint one man to act as a sort of head water man for their lateral. The farmer who has the forty acres of alfalfa which he wants irrigated goes to see this head water man. If the other farmers are ready the gate tender opens the headgate to the lateral, the water flows down the lateral and each man uses the whole stream for a certain time and then passes it on to the next man. Each farmer has a sub-lateral and from it the water is passed on to the field. Now, here is our man with forty acres of alfalfa. The water has come down the main canal; the gate tender has turned it into the lateral by opening the gate, and our man has turned the water into the little lateral on his farm; the water is flowing here right along the upper side of his alfalfa field. This field has a border of dirt every four to six rods. The farmer takes his spade and lets the water into one or two of the spaces between the borders. After the water covers everything between these border spaces he closes the opening and goes to the next and lets in the water. In other words, he floods each section of his field in this way. With fruit and melons we use furrow irrigation. We let each man have water by the hour. Here is one man who has twice as many acres as another. He gets the water just twice as long; that is the general scheme."

This man has been raised in the Salt River valley and was very optimistic about the government work. "Right now," he said, "is the lowest time of the year, but even though the storage dam is not working, we are giving the people more water than they ever got before at this season. Some of them are complaining, but that is because they expected the storage dam to be working this year. We gave them this month 22,000 miner's inches and that is more than they ever got under the old system." A miner's inch is a flow of water of one-fortieth of a cubic foot per second. It is reckoned that each quarter section should have sixty-four miner's inches. The 22,000 miner's inches, therefore, would supply only 60,000 acres. There has always been a shortage of water during the summer months, and it is to overcome this that the storage dam at Roosevelt is being built.

The gate keeper showed me the provision for cleaning out sediment. A settling basin is provided—a sharp incline in one side of the canal. When the settling basin is full the sediment is shot out at the side. I talked with the wife of the gate keeper. She was a former Illinois lady, and enjoyed telling me how frightened new-comers were of the various animals and reptiles. "Why, sir," she said, "whenever I see a rattlesnake or a scorpion or a centipede or a Gila monster or a tarantula or anything of that sort I just stop and kill it, and don't think anything about it. A night or so ago we were sleeping out doors. A rattler came rattling along just in front of the bed. My husband just picked up a chair and killed it, and didn't think a thing about it. A year or so ago a scorpion crawled up my sleeve and stung me; it paralyzed my arm to the shoulder, but I didn't mind it much. Whenever you sleep out of doors here you always want to shake out your bedding. I knew a young man who got bit by a sidewinder because he forgot it. Sidewinders are little things worse than rattlesnakes."

I asked the lady how she liked the country compared

with Illinois. "Oh, I like it splendidly," she said; "I wouldn't go back to Illinois for anything."

That afternoon I walked back to Mesa and took the Southern Pacific for Phoenix, and that night left the Salt River valley. It is a very interesting valley and when the government irrigation scheme is in good working order it will fill up rapidly with quarter section farmers who will make a lot of money. But I was not sorry to leave. The sun is very hot there.

⁊ V ⁊

California—A Misunderstood State

Say California, and the easterner immediately thinks of orange groves, balmy breezes, wonderful fruit, and Los Angeles. He may go further and picture in his mind the mountains and the ocean beaches. He has heard of California. Oh yes; he has heard of California for years. California has made a great noise in the world, and Californians are great advertisers. California is the best advertised state in the union. And yet the real California is quite unknown east of the Rockies.

When I came to California I had the thought in mind that I was going to have a little pleasure, and rest up before I got into more agricultural land which I must investigate. I was mistaken; much mistaken. California's agricultural possibilities are far beyond those of any country which I have yet seen on my trip. I was prepared to see several thousand acres of wonderful orange groves kept in beautiful shape and supporting a thick population, but I was not prepared to see a true agricultural country several million acres in extent, as yet but little developed.

Our eastern idea of California is Los Angeles and the surrounding territory. The Los Angeles country is wonderful. But Los Angeles thinks she's "It"—thinks she and her

Note: The first part of chapter 5, on Southern California, was published in *Wallaces' Farmer,* August 13, 1909.

surrounding fruit land are California. At least this is the impression I got.

Los Angeles and southern California are not California; in fact, but a very small though wonderfully attractive part. To get any clear general idea of agricultural California you must study the map a little. If you remember your school days geography you will remember there are two ranges of mountains in California, the coast range and the Sierra Nevada. In between these two ranges and extending north and south for 500 miles is a great valley, averaging forty miles in width. This valley running lengthwise through central California is the true agricultural California. The valley is divided into two parts; named after the rivers which formed them, the Sacramento and the San Joaquin (Whakeen). The whole big valley contains 10,000,000 acres, 2,000,000 in the northern division or the Sacramento and the remainder in the San Joaquin. The area of this great agricultural valley is two-sevenths of the area of Iowa.

The southern California country so familiar to us extends from Santa Barbara on the north to the Mexican boundary line on the south. This strip is about 170 miles long and varies from thirty to sixty miles in breadth. Around the rivers where irrigation is possible is the great orange and lemon country. There are 120,000 acres in oranges and lemons. The citrus fruit country of the south California valley is located very largely in the close vicinity of Los Angeles.

South on the great Salton Sea, in the southeast corner of California, is the Imperial valley, a great irrigated country. At most there will be but 400,000 acres of agricultural land here.

Besides the Great Inland valley, the Southern California valley, and the Imperial valley, there is a scattering of agricultural land along the coast and a few inland rivers. The rest of the state is mostly mountainous and absolutely unfit for agriculture. The majority of the agricultural land of the state is in the great inland valleys of the Sacramento and San Joaquin.

It is hard work to struggle through a bunch of statistics and geography, but to begin to understand what sort of a state California really is it is absolutely necessary.

My first impression of California wasn't very pleasant. It was about 5 o'clock in the afternoon when our train crossed the Colorado river from Arizona. It was very hot. At either end of the car electric fans were going, and all of the windows were shut to keep out the dry, hot desert wind; yet the thermometer in the car registered 104 degrees.

Instead of the California you read about of oranges and palms, there was a wide, barren sand desert. It stretched glaringly away under the hot sun with bunches of sage brush and cactus here and there. We climbed on through this "howling wilderness" all night, but when I awoke the next morning the scene had changed absolutely. The first thing I saw was an orange grove. From the most barren land possible we had come to the most highly cultivated land in the world. This is typical of California. She likes to present surprises at every turn. For many miles we rolled through orange groves. Occasionally right next to a beautifully kept grove I would see a stretch of semi-desert, a sample of how all the orange land looked before irrigation. This land had a thick covering of big rocks washed down

Irrigation on a California date ranch (Seaver Center for Western History Research, Natural History Museum of Los Angeles County).

from the hills. There was a thin scattering of scrubby live oak in dark green gnarledness. Without prospect of water such land is worth practically nothing. With irrigation it becomes, with a bearing grove on it, worth as much as $2,500 an acre. Fifteen hundred dollars an acre for an orange grove is fairly low as a quoted price. Work and water have converted one of the most barren wastes into one of the most beautiful and productive countries in the world.

Through this beautiful country towns are thickly scattered. I left the train at one of these little towns, Upland, about forty miles out of Los Angeles. A friend took me to see the country. Upland has one main avenue seven miles long, a street car line running the entire length. The avenue is a broad oiled road lined with graceful pepper trees. The street car track has a line of pepper trees immediately on either side of it. Then comes the oiled road and then the last line of pepper trees. The car ran up a steep grade to the foothills. As we ran up I noticed one continual line of orange groves; grove after grove of little bushy green trees.

All these groves were kept in perfect shape; not a blade of grass nor a weed could I see. A perfect dust mulch covered all the grove floors. This perfect order continued for several miles with houses scattered here and there every few blocks. The houses are of the low California style, and the grounds are beautifully kept. I hardly knew whether I was in town or country. These houses are in the town of Upland and derive their income from the orange groves, five to ten acres in extent. This appealed to me as an ideal combination of country and town advantages.

We ran on up in the car till we reached the foothills at the base of the mountains. Here what a wonderful view we had! Below us spread out a large part of the great valley of southern California. Close at hand spread out the long, level floor of orange groves. On further the original barren desert untouched by water. Then a little further on oranges again, here and there in the midst of which would be a little town nestling. For miles and miles the valley was checkered with orange groves.

On a clear day from this vantage point I was told that Catalina Island could be seen, 100 miles away. A generation ago looking down on this scene I would have seen a barren waste. Now I saw the wide level floor of the valley spreading on for sixty or seventy miles, dotted with orange groves, peaches, apricots, vineyards, and walnuts. My friend told me that in the far distance was a true farming land of sugar beets, alfalfa, and stock raising.

We took the car down from the foothills. The electric power is developed by the mountain streams, which are afterward used for irrigation. Formerly this car line was mule-propelled, and here was the place where the mules hauled the car up the slope and then were taken on the rear platform and the car coasted down.

I was taken on a beautiful automobile drive over the country surrounding Upland. The roads were fine where oiled, but where not oiled they were extremely dusty. We drove through several pretty little towns with palm or pepper tree avenues; through grove after grove of beautifully kept oranges. Then getting down lower into the valley we passed through peach and apricot orchards. These are not kept in as nice shape as the orange groves. We passed through a mile or so of vineyards, kept in fine shape. The ground is perfectly cultivated. Every year the vines are cut down to a stub and the new growth which springs out bears the grapes. According to variety, the grapes are used for raisins, wine, or table. I was told that the oranges were grown more around the foothills where there was less likelihood of frost, more water, and a gravelly soil well adapted to oranges.

We drove down a long avenue of stately eucalyptus trees forty or fifty feet high. My friend told me that they were about five years old. They were now of good size for fire wood. My friend warned me against the eucalyptus proposition. "The eucalyptus," he told me, "is a wonderful tree; produces fire wood in four years from planting; springs

Irrigation of orange groves, Los Angeles County, circa 1910 (Security Pacific National Bank Photograph Collection, Los Angeles Public Library).

up from the stump when cut down, and in four years produces another crop of fire wood; makes excellent hard wood for finishing; and should be a good paying crop in California on the cheaper land." "But," he said, "there is not a single grove to my knowledge in profitable operation as yet. It may have a great future, but it's being boomed too much now and someone's going to get caught."

I visited several of the small towns in the vicinity of Los Angeles and found them all much the same. Each vies with the other in claiming the prettiest location, most comfortable climate, best orange land, etc. All these little towns with their surrounding fruit and farming

Hauling water to irrigate trees in the San Fernando valley (Security Pacific National Bank Photograph Collection, Los Angeles Public Library).

land are wonderfully beautiful. In fact, advantages are heaped one on top of the other till you almost think it is a paradise.

But there are drawbacks. The land is very high in price. Land with a bearing orange grove is held at from $1,500 an acre up; $2,000 an acre isn't thought high. "Why," they will tell you, "you can make great interest on your money with land at that rate." Then they will invariably wander off into some tale of a man in the vicinity who made $400 net profit per acre on his orange grove; 20 per cent interest on land at $2,000 an acre. I heard similar tales a score of times.

Then I got hold of some unprejudiced people and tried to get next to some of the drawbacks. There are many of them. For one thing, the climate often steps in and spoils things. A frost will often put a crop pretty well to the bad. There are lines of frost through the country. Orange groves at a certain height will escape from frost while those at a lower height may get caught.

Very hot weather is also bad, and almost an entire orange crop will be caused to drop because of a hot spell just after a cold one.

Then there are fungus diseases, among the worst of which are the scales. Nearly all orange trees in California are attacked. To prevent scale, fumigation with cyanide gas is practiced everywhere.

Besides all this there is a labor problem, and it is a big one. White laborers are few. The Japs are good, but are intensely disliked and not reliable when working by the day. They are very good workmen when they work for themselves or by the job.

Then an orange grove requires the highest type of cultivation. It must be irrigated three or four times during the summer, and after each irrigation perfect cultivation must be given. The trees must be fertilized about once a year. Nitrogenous fertilizers like tankage, guano, and nitrate of soda are used. The expense for fertilizer runs around $50 a year per acre. Very great care must be taken in picking the fruit. The fruit is picked by clipping the stems. The stem must be clipped, but the skin must not be punctured or rot will set in later.

All of this means that the very highest type of farming must be practiced. And it is, for farming here is a fine art. There is lots of work and care necessary, but the work is clean and enjoyable and quite well distributed over the year, so that there is an absence of grinding toil.

Neighbors are close at hand. Life flows along easily, for the climate doesn't vary much. In the winter it gets a little cooler and the rainy season comes on. In the summer the bright days flow on without interruption. Sometimes the thermometer runs over 100, but a tempering breeze blows in every day from the ocean. Nearly every morning a mist from the ocean hangs over the country far to the inland, but this melts away under the sun of the late forenoon.

I envied these orange people with their beautiful surroundings and their attractive business with its spice of uncertainty. There are enough difficulties and technicalities in the business to keep the faculties bright. The methods of irrigation with their peculiarities as adapted to soil and slope, the intense cultivation, the protection from frost, the fertilizing, the fumigation, the careful picking and packing, and last of all the successful marketing, are all details which sharpen the wits of the orange man. And it necessarily follows that with such intense cultivation and such dense population the type of people is of the highest. No mossbacks can survive. They have not that fear of co-operation which so marks our eastern farmers. This is partly due to the fact that co-operation is a necessity with them. It was formerly a case of "all hang together or all hang separately." Oranges were sold to shippers at such low prices that the business became unprofitable. Many of the orange men were formerly business men and, knowing the value of co-operation, got together, formed a fruit marketing association, marketed their own fruit, and made money. The story of this association is so interesting and instructive to us of the middle west who are bungling with our co-operative associations that I am going to devote an entire article to it later.

Of course orange growing is not the only industry of southern California, but it is the distinguishing industry, and the one in which southern California leads. There is also deciduous fruit growing, market gardening, grape growing, walnut growing, and some alfalfa and grains. A peculiar thing about it all is the fact that each crop has a certain strip or area given over to it. Practice shows that each locality has some particular crop which it is best adapted to. So all of the people get together and raise this one crop and reap the advantages which come from all people of a locality being interested in the same industry. Rotation is not practiced and of necessity can not be practiced with fruit trees.

Southern California is a wonderfully attractive place, but it is not the place where the average Iowa farmer can invest his money to advantage. It is the ideal place for the man in broken health with plenty of money to come and live. For the young man with little money openings are rather slim. It takes a long time to get a good start. If I had thought southern California to be a land offering opportunities to the average Iowa farmer, I would have described it in detail, but as it is I have merely given a surface view. Next week I will tell of my trip through northern California.

California's San Joaquin Valley

From Los Angeles and the southern California country I went north into the San Joaquin valley. I stopped first at Bakersfield, about 150 miles north of Los Angeles, in the southern part of the valley of the San Joaquin river. Here conditions are peculiar, due to the fact that so much land is held in two large estates of several hundred thousand acres each.

The first thing I did in Bakersfield was to hunt up Mr. Jastro, president of the American Live Stock Association and manager of the Kern County Land Company. When he found that I had but a day to spend in seeing the country around Bakersfield he threw up his hands in dismay.

"Why," he said, "you can not more than get the beginning of an idea about this country in that time."

Then he started to give me a slight idea of the country before he sent me out for myself. The first thing he impressed upon me was the fact that it is one of the biggest irrigation propositions to be found anywhere. For crops alfalfa, wheat, and barley are the biggest; although now it is quite a fruit country, and in time will be greater. The cattle feeding proposition is one of the biggest industries of the valley. The cattle are brought in from Arizona and New Mexico and are finished off on the native pasture, alfalfa hay, and sometimes some Kaffir corn or barley.

He told me that the labor problem was one of the big difficulties with which they had to deal. I was so absent-

Note: The sections on California's San Joaquin and Sacramento valleys were published in *Wallaces' Farmer,* August 20, 1909.

minded as to mention Japanese to him, and it was like touching a match to a powder mine. The Japanese are "conceited, utterly unreliable, without a trace of business morality, and poor workmen except when working for themselves."

In order to overcome the labor difficulties in the valley the big companies use many labor-saving contrivances. This is a country where big harvesters are used, hauled by twenty or thirty horses. Now the horses are being replaced by big oil-burning steam engines. All this and much more he told me, and then sent me out with Mr. Sanders, one of his cattlemen, to see the country for myself.

It was 10 o'clock in the morning when I climbed into an open buggy with Mr. Sanders behind a pair of pintos. We drove out of Bakersfield on a smooth, level, hard, oiled road. Mr. Sanders told me that such roads ran out in all directions from Bakersfield for eight to sixteen miles. Such roads as these are a great blessing to any country.

We had gone but a short distance when houses became few and far between. We passed many ill kept alfalfa fields. They were weedy, of uneven stand, and showed badly the lack of water. Many of the fields were being pastured closely and the alfalfa showed the effects in the uneven stand.

The ground spread out quite level across the valley, broken here and there by lines of trees along the irrigating ditches, to the lines of mountains on all sides twenty, thirty, and forty miles away.

We drove along behind the pintos at a good sharp gait until we were three or four miles from town, when we turned in at what Mr. Sanders assured me was the show

A combined harvester and thresher in a California wheat field (Wallaces' Farmer, August 20, 1909)

place of the whole country. From what I could see from the driveway it was a jumble of trees and shrubs hiding a rambling ranch house.

Mr. Sanders said: "Climb down and we'll take a look over the place here just to show you what can be done with this soil and climate."

We walked in and out along paths between tall, thick bamboos. Some were six inches in diameter and thirty feet high. This was truly tropical. Then we wound out into a more open space. Here was a blue grass lawn planted with elm trees and many beautiful tropical shrubs and trees of which I did not know the names. Then there were ornamental orange trees with their dark green leaves and golden fruit scattered over the blue grass. Blue grass is rare in this country and I always appreciate the sight of it. It was a truly beautiful sight, the open blue grass lawn flanked with trees and the curving gravel walks, perfectly trimmed, winding in and out amongst shrubbery and bamboo. To add to the beauty there were many birds singing in the trees and shrubs. It seemed like a garden of an Arabian Nights tale.

Leaving this scene, we drove on down the oiled road. The excellence of the oiled road contrasted strongly with the lack of settlement. No more houses were to be seen. Yet all this land was under irrigation. Most of the fields were in a mixture of alfalfa and weeds. We drove alongside an irrigating ditch partly silted up and with weeds and shrubs growing along the side. All this land showed badly the need of care.

It grew hotter and hotter, yet Mr. Sanders assured me that this wasn't hot for Bakersfield. He reckoned the heat to be only about 97 degrees, yet the pintos trotted steadily along and were not even sweating.

As we got out further the land became more rolling and consequently more difficult to irrigate. Either it must be leveled or it must be handled with contour checks. Here contour checks are used; that is, ridges are thrown up, connecting land of the same height. The alfalfa fields which I saw presented a fantastic appearance. Winding smoke-like in and out among the alfalfa field were long low levees. These levees divide the field into plots or checks of from one to five or six or even more acres in extent. All this plot will have nearly the same elevation.

The division of land into large plots is especially adapted to conditions like those at Bakersfield, where a large amount of water must be handled in a short time. Mr. Sanders told me that when the snows in the mountains were melting fast that their main canal would be flowing nearly 1,000 second feet of water. To use this before it runs away to waste is the problem. Therefore the land is divided into large checks into which the water can be poured in a hurry.

Of course such a hasty use of water means lots of waste. Several places in the road were flooded with waste irrigation water. Moreover, such hasty use means that some of the alfalfa at the lower ends of the checks will be killed out with too much water and some of it at the upper ends won't get enough. But the water comes with such a rush down from the mountains during such a short period of time that no other system than the large check is very practicable just now. A crying need in the valley is a storage reservoir up in the mountains where the Kern river heads, from which most irrigation water is obtained. A storage reservoir would store up the flood water against the time of need. As it is, when water is plentiful it is spread on thick everywhere and a great deal of damage is done. Then later when water is scarce more damage results from the lack of it. It appeared to me that irrigation is great here on account of future possibilities rather than what has already been done. Yet Mr. Sanders told me that there are 1,500 miles of irrigation ditches and around 200,000 acres of land under irrigation. It's a big irrigation proposition, but as yet it is very crude.

We has passed from the smooth oiled road to a dusty sand road. No houses were in sight. All this land is owned by the Kern County Land Company. As we drove along I noticed a few bunches of Hereford steers grazing on some of the scraggly looking alfalfa. These steers, Mr. Sanders told me, had been shipped in from New Mexico and were being finished on alfalfa for the California market.

I commented several times on the poor appearance of the alfalfa to Mr. Sanders. He explained this by the fact that the Kern County Land Company had been devoting its energies to the raising of grain on some fine new bottom land and had no extra help to keep the alfalfa up in shape.

"Why sir," he said to me, "this is one of the finest alfalfa countries in the world—five, six, and seven cuttings a year. But then, you see, we've been neglecting the alfalfa for the last three or four years and the weeds are taking it bad."

As we drove on further we saw a few very nice fields of alfalfa which were being cut for the third time. For a strip of ten miles and more we saw no houses. Nearly all the land in the valley belongs to the Kern County Land Company and to Mr. Miller. Besides these two companies there

94

are a few, a very few, settlers. These companies are slow about selling. They advertise but little and only sell their land a little at a time around the edges. The irrigated land is held at an average of about $80 an acre, but there is not much for sale.

We passed now through a small strip of alkali on which there was little else than salt grass growing. "Through the valley," Mr. Sanders told me, "there were several strips of alkali both white and black which must be carefully avoided."

At length we reached a long, level stretch of grain country. This was a lake bottom about fifteen years ago. Now it is in broad, level fields of the most beautiful grain that I have ever seen. The fields were yellow, perfectly level, and stretched away beautifully for miles. I remember one wheat field. The straw was shoulder-high and the stand perfect. In the distance I could see the steam harvesters working on the barley. While we drove over to them Mr. Sanders told me a little about their wheat growing.

This lake bottom land had been in wheat for seven years continuously and had yielded at the rate of twenty-three to thirty sacks (each sack weighs 140 pounds) to the acre each year.

"What," I said, "forty-five to sixty bushels to the acre?"

"That's what," he told me. "And one year on a section the growth was so rank in the early spring that we pastured it down for several weeks with a thousand head of cattle, then got twenty-seven sacks to the acre, and there was enough seed left on the ground to self-sow it and the next year we got twenty-seven sacks to the acre again."

I looked at Mr. Sanders a little incredulously and he

looked at me sorrowfully and said: "Yes, I know when we tell tales like that back east they won't believe us, but it's true, just the same."

For one thing here the wheat is not the same quality as our eastern wheat. It is big grained and fairly white and soft.

Then we reached the harvester. It was walking right along at two and one-half or three miles an hour. Behind it vomited forth straw. On one side it was cutting a twenty-foot swath of grain. On top of the harvester were a couple of men handling the grain sacks as they were filled and sending them down a chute at the side which dumped the sacks onto the ground when ten sacks were filled. These sacks were picked up by a man and wagon and hauled to the cars on a spur of the railroad near by. Besides the two sack tenders there was an engineer and fireman for the steam traction engine and two other men who helped generally, making six men in all.

It was just a little impressive to see that tremendous machine walk right along cutting the grain and dumping it out sacked in the field at the rate of forty acres to the day.

Methods of culture are simple. The ground is plowed; the wheat is harrowed in; and along in the spring an irrigation is given. The plowing is done by steam. Then in July the wheat is harvested by steam. Expense is small; returns are large. But this is not true farming, and can not go on always. Wonderful though this old lake bottom soil is, it will wear out if kept much longer in wheat. Other California land has gone through the same process. Land which once yielded fifty bushels to the acre now yields ten and twenty bushels.

I looked at this soil carefully. It is gray in color and looks very limey. It has quite a bit of sand, and clods break quite easily. The company had some 5,000 acres in grain. We drove on past this to the headquarters for this ranch. This was a beautiful little place, a low, rambling ranch house with a magnificent blue grass lawn covered with trees. I noticed several fig trees.

Mr. Connor, the manager of the ranch, is one of the greatest irrigation enthusiasts to be found anywhere. He is an enthusiastic believer in the possibilities of the San Joaquin valley. He points to Los Angeles and then says: "What they have done, we can do, and more. We can raise just as good fruit and we've better soil. What we have got to do is to solve the water problem. And right here, young man, is tremendous opportunity; but it will take the government to handle it right. No private concern or cooperation can do it. It will take millions of dollars to build a storage reservoir up in the mountains and then spread the water rightly over the land."

"I suppose, young man," said Mr. Connor, addressing me, "that one of the things you've most noticed here is the lack of people."

I assented, for in the course of the whole drive of over thirty miles I had seen but three or four houses, but four or five people, and but two teams.

I enjoyed Mr. Connor immensely, for he is a frank, open-hearted man with tremendous faith in Kern county and its future. He has thought long and hard about irrigation methods and for over an hour he talked and diagrammed to me systems of irrigation. Then evening fell.

We went to dinner. I say dinner because it was served

in dinner style. A noiseless Chinee served us with three courses. All the cooking out here, they tell me, is done by Chinamen.

The meal over, Mr. Sanders drove with me back to town. It was in the cool of the evening. The sun had set in red glory behind the mountains at the end of the valley and had left a dull red afterglow.

It was nearly twenty miles to town and during the whole drive we met no team, and until we got close to town I saw no sign of life or human habitation anywhere.

In town I bade goodbye to Mr. Sanders and waited for my midnight train, and as I waited I thought of the possibilities of the great valley. Here is a valley of over a half million acres with 200,000 under irrigation, yet practically unsettled. With just as good a climate for fruit as is to be found in California, yet only a few scattering orchards, ill kept. What the valley needs is people.

I caught the midnight train and passed up north through the San Joaquin valley to San Francisco. From San Francisco I went to Sacramento.

Here at Sacramento I met Mr. W. A. Beard, a member of the Country Life Commission and editor of the *Great West.* He is wonderfully enthusiastic over the Sacramento valley and its future. It is his dream to see the whole valley reclaimed and irrigated.

Sacramento Valley

When he found that I knew practically nothing as yet about the valley he talked steadily to me for three and a half hours on California, and especially on Sacramento and her possibilities. He got a map of the state; showed me the two

98

mountain ranges with the valley in between. Then he explained that the temperature is a great deal the same throughout the valley, that oranges will ripen just as well and just as early at Oroville, 100 miles north of San Francisco, as they will down in the Los Angeles orange country, 400 and 500 miles south of San Francisco. In fact, the same isothermal line connects southern California and the San Joaquin and Sacramento valleys. Then he explained rainfall. During the summer there is practically no rain. In the winter there is the rainy season. The southern California has but little rainfall even in winter. As you come north the rainfall increases.

Then he told me of crops and possibilities. There are 2,000,000 acres in the Sacramento valley which are subject to irrigation. This is a wonderful fruit country, but probably the great crop of the valley will be alfalfa. Five to seven cuttings can be made a year. Great possibilities are open in dairying and feeding in connection with alfalfa growing. Much feeding is now being done with cattle brought down from the hills. These cattle are simply finished on alfalfa alone.

In the past the Sacramento valley was one of the greatest wheat sections in the United States. Wheat was raised on a bonanza scale year after year. Great profits were made. Then failure followed. Production fell from forty and fifty bushels to less than twenty. Irrigation was not needed for the wheat because of the heavy winter rains. Expenses were low, little labor was needed, and the natural result was large holdings.

Now with the failure of wheat farming irrigation is slowly coming in. The large holdings have fought it. The crazy water laws of the state have worked against it; but irrigation is here now, and here to stay.

In the future holdings will be small, forty acres or less. Alfalfa will be the big crop. It runs very often ten tons to the acre, and at the same time is building up the soil. Market gardening and fruit also will be big crops.

Then he told me about the big Sacramento floods. Nearly every winter the Sacramento overflows. Last winter it covered a million acres, or nearly half the valley. But the government is at work now building levees to control it.

He talked till my head swam with the wonders and possibilities and problems of the Sacramento valley.

After the talk he took me for a walk. He showed me the Capitol Park. This is truly a beauty. There are thirty-five acres of it, and on it he told me is the most complete collection of trees to be found anywhere. I saw oranges, ornamental palms, date palms, elms, oaks, ash, and all our northern trees, pines of all sorts, spruces, cedars, etc., etc, ad infinitum. There were several species of the Sequoia and giant red wood. There was one large spot on which was a tree brought from each battlefield of the Civil war. I stopped and read the label attached to each tree—Fair Oaks, Chancellorsville, Gettysburg, etc. Oaks, elms, maples, lindens, our eastern trees, there were. Around the edges of the park is a line of wonderfully striking pines, the rock pine. I call them the hard maple of the evergreen family, for they are broad, bushy, and not conical like most conifers. Over the whole park is the thick velvety sod of Bermuda grass, and nowhere are any signs to keep off.

It was Sabbath afternoon, and all over the park people

were scattered. The capitol building was rather a disappointment. It is not nearly so fine as the Iowa state house.

My day at Sacramento over, I took the train north along the valley. I traveled by day as I wanted to see a bit of this wonderful valley. What I saw from the train was mainly long stretches of grain fields with here and there orchards and vineyards and some alfalfa fields. Nearer the river were long stretches of marshy land and the train crossed several long stretches of several miles of tule water left from the floods of last January.

I had a spare afternoon to spend in the valley and spent it at Gridley. I met here an old Ames graduate, Edgar Stanton, a son of Prof. E. W. Stanton. He is in the irrigation engineering business. He took me for a long ride over the country. We passed a long series of grain fields. These were owned, Mr. Stanton told me, by a man who owned several thousand acres, none of which were under irrigation. This man was living easy and didn't believe in irrigation. Such men are holding the country back badly. Of course they can't hold 1,000 acres and irrigate it themselves, but they could sell most of it to be irrigated and the land would support eight or ten families where it now supports one.

Mr. Stanton told me that grain growing is becoming less and less each year. Alfalfa and irrigation are replacing it. I saw long, broad fields of alfalfa of the first class. The country here spreads beautifully level to the mountain ranges on either side of the valley. It is nicely adapted to irrigation.

I saw several peach orchards, one of which is said to be the largest in the state. A good orchard in full bearing should net $150 to the acre. I saw a fig orchard and prunes, plums, pears and apricots. These orchards were not kept in the beautiful shape of those of southern California, but they were loaded with fruit just the same. Some of the orchards in the lower valley were unirrigated. Others, higher up, were irrigated.

I didn't see any orange groves, but was told on reliable authority time and again that oranges are successfully grown in the valley and may be marketed a month earlier than the southern California orange.

The alfalfa here yields four to six cuttings. The hay sells at from $6 to $12 a ton. Last year $12 a ton was reached. Mr. Stanton told me that one of the nicest propositions in the valley was a big alfalfa ranch with cattle feeding in connection.

But there is a dark side to this country. As Mr. Stanton said to me: "This country looks rosy to you now, but I could paint it black and blue in the face. Many people have failed here and moved away."

The chaotic condition of irrigation laws, the inability oftentimes to get water when it is most needed, and the terrific winter floods combine to make a dark picture. Over half the thirty-mile drive was over country covered last winter by the flood. Now it looks pleasant with its fruit trees and alfalfa fields.

The cost of land subject to irrigation now but not yet leveled and checked is from $70 to $100. The cost of leveling, checking, and seeding to alfalfa runs about $20 an acre. Mr. Stanton was contracting for precisely this work at $18 to $20 an acre. He told me that careful leveling of the ground was one of the most important requisites of success in alfalfa growing. Man after man had failed because he feared the expense of doing the job right.

The system of irrigation here is the check system. The field is divided by little levees into checks of less than an acre each. Each check has its gate on the field ditch. This makes irrigation simple if the leveling has been done right. The gate for each check is opened and the operator watches the water do the work.

I left California that night. I went to California with an erroneous impression, thinking that there was not much to see in an agricultural line. Probably she has the biggest agricultural prospects of any state in the Rockies or west. I had only allotted a short time to California and merely had time to take a superficial glance at her great valleys.

One of the things which impressed me about all of California was the opportunities for amusement and social life for the farmer. A mountain outing is easily taken and, I noticed, is often used. The sea coast is not far away, and offers more opportunities for amusement. Outdoor life the year round, closeness to mountain and seaside resorts, hunting and fishing, add greatly to the value of California even to the farmer. And the farmers avail themselves of these advantages here as nowhere else in the United States.

In the words of Prof. Elwood Mead, of the United States Department of Agriculture:

"Southern California has demonstrated the value of irrigation. Northern California illustrates its latent possibilities when one considers the vast area of the Sacramento and San Joaquin valleys with a surface sloped by nature for the easy spreading of water; with a soil of great fertility, and a marvelous climate, there is no doubt but that it is to be during the twentieth century a great field of activity, not of the farmer alone, but of the engineer, the lawyer, and the student of social and economic questions. The available water supply of this valley ought to make it the Egypt of the Western Hemisphere."

ᔷᐧ VI ᔷᐧ

The Government Irrigation Project at Umatilla, Oregon

The Umatilla project is in northeastern Oregon, where the Umatilla river meets the Columbia. This project is only 22,000 acres in extent. It presents many peculiarities which make it extremely interesting. Last year the government irrigation works were completed but the country as yet is practically undeveloped. Sage brush still holds sway over the largest part of the project. Yet this land, growing practically nothing now, is said by the government experts to be wonderful fruit land.

It was 1 o'clock in the morning when I stepped off the train at Hermiston, the central town of the Umatilla project. It was a relief to feel the cool, dry breeze after the moist air of the coast. Scarcely had I landed at Hermiston when two hotel men were clamoring for my baggage. This competition I found to be rather typical of the town.

The next morning I awoke and looked out on a cloudy atmosphere. At the breakfast table the cloudiness was greatly commented on. The gentleman to my left told me that cloudy days were unusual during the summer; that summer rain was almost unknown and that, in fact, the yearly rainfall was only about eight inches.

Breakfast over, I walked down the main street of Her-

Note: Chapter 6, "The Government Irrigation Project at Umatilla, Oregon," was published in *Wallaces' Farmer,* August 27, 1909.

miston. The town is a live one. It was founded only three years ago. Now it has a population of 1,000. I saw two excellent hotels, too many and too good for the size of the place. There are several new concrete buildings and a couple of blocks of fairly decent brick store buildings. But the town looks ungainly—sprawled over the desert. There are absolutely no trees and no grass. The main street is inches deep in fine sand. It seemed to me the place looked desolate, but the inhabitants thought it was a marvel of up-to-date improvements. And they are right, when the length of time it has been founded is considered.

I stopped at a real estate office to get the land men's opinion of the country before I went out to see for myself.

I said: "If an Iowa man came out here with $1,500 what sort of a go could he make of it?"

"Well," the land man said, "your man ought to have more money; yet if he was a hard worker and a sticker he could pull through in good shape. What he would want to do would be to buy ten acres of land—that's going to be plenty in this country for any man; going to be great fruit country here, you know. This would cost him $150 an acre, one-fifth down. Land at this price is uncleared and not ready yet for water. As soon as it can be cleared, leveled, and ditches put in government water can be secured. The cost of water is a maintenance cost of $1 an acre and $6 an acre every year for ten years to pay for the cost of the government works. This would make the cost per acre, itemized as follows:

Irrigation Project at Umatilla, Oregon

Original cost	$150
Cost of irrigation project,	
$6 per year for ten years	60
Clearing and leveling, $3 to $75	
per acre, probably average	40
Total cost per acre	$250

"To this must be added a yearly maintenance tax of $1 per acre, and if set in fruit, the original cost of the trees. Your Iowa man would have to pay something like $300 down on his ten acres the first year; he would have to pay $70 on the ten acres to the government the first year. Besides this he would have to lay out expense and labor in getting his land in shape. The first year he couldn't make enough to support him. He would have to fall back on his $1,500. The second year he ought to break even. All the time he would be clearing his land, seeding it, and gradually getting it into orchards.

"Oh, it takes a man with plenty of nerve and grit to stick by that sort of a proposition, I tell you. But he's going to get his reward. Look at the Yakima country and the Hood river country. Land there at first was just the same as this. Now bearing orchards are selling at $1,000 to $2,500 an acre. The government says all this country will be like that some day. Government analyses show we have the same soil. Our climate is the same and our water supply is better."

I thanked this man and went out to see the country for myself. The project is comparatively small, so I thought I might get a good idea of it by going on foot. I started out northeast of Hermiston on a deep sandy road. Immediately out of town the sage brush began and the valley rolled away up and down in gray greenness to the hills of the Columbia and Umatilla rivers. Over this gray rolling plain were scattered a few unpainted houses.

The sand road was hard walking; it was like walking in a six-inch snow. Around the lea of a little knoll the sand was drifted three and four feet high through the sage brush. The wind was blowing hard and filling the air with fine sand. The sand is rather a gray buff color, and gray was the color of the horizon, and gray was the sage brush plain. And my idea of the country was slightly gray.

Close to town I noticed an acre or so in healthy, growing young apple switches—evidently planted this spring. Also there was a half acre or so in grape vines. There is no trouble in getting a dust mulch on this land. In fact, the wind furnishes a fine sand mulch gratis. There are no weeds

Sagebrush and sand: typical undeveloped land on the Umatilla project (Wallaces' Farmer, *August 27, 1909)*

to bother, as none except the Russian thistle and a few of its kindred are hardy enough to bother this country in its present state.

A little further on I noticed a man working hard with a mattock digging out sage brush. The brush was three or four feet high and looked tough and gnarled.

The gray sand road led up and down over the rolling rises and wound in and out between the everlasting gray-green sage brush. I passed several unpainted one or two-room houses and one or two tents, but saw no people. Then I passed an irrigation ditch and on a bit further on top of a little knoll I saw two men irrigating the bare land just cleared of sage brush. I watched them a short time to catch their method. A little ditch full of water came winding around on the high hill ground from the big ditch. The water was bridged across a couple of low places by wooden flumes. The sand sides of the ditch where the men were irrigating had a lath box made by nailing four laths together every four feet or so. These little lath boxes were to bring the water out of the ditch and were about eighteen feet long and perforated the sides of the ditch about eight inches above the bottom. As the water came down the ditch it ran out each of these little boxes and from the boxes was carried away by furrows. Each box had three furrows to supply, which made the furrows about every eighteen inches. The ditch was on the high ground and the land sloped each way so the little streams of water ran nicely down each furrow.

I asked one of the men why he was irrigating the dry ground. He said:

"We just sowed rye here."

"Why," I said, "I can't see why you grow a crop like rye on this land."

"Well," said he, "you see it's this way. After the sage brush is cleared off there's nothing to hold the soil, and with these heavy winds here we're liable to lose the top six inches of our soil. Now, rye is the best crop we have to stand the wind and hold the land till we can get it into alfalfa and then fruit trees."

I could see the purpose of rye easily just then, for the wind was blowing in gusts and the air was filled with sand.

On a little further I saw a right nice little house and decided to see what my chances were for dinner. A large, fleshy German woman was in the garden tugging at a little check gate in her ditch to let the water go on down and not flood her garden any more. I asked this woman if I could get dinner there and she said, "Yes, if you are willing to take what I get." So I stayed and she went in to get dinner. She and her little daughter were alone; her husband was off in the mountains.

While she was getting dinner I talked with her. "We've got ten acres here," she said. "Just got here last fall and built the barn and lived in it last winter. My, but it was cold! It went down a little under zero once or twice. Old timers said it was the coldest since back in the eighties. Lots of people got their potatoes froze. We built the house in early spring and we built it tight too. We don't want dust."

"We like it fine here. The worst thing about the country is the big sand storms. It just gets awful in the summer, and it's so hard for a woman to keep a house clean. Why, the sand just lies in the window sills in drifts. It makes some women so nervous, you know, to have the sand all over everything. I got so I didn't mind it so much; it's clean dirt, you know; but thank goodness this house is built tight."

"Then it's a bit lonely here and we're sort of breaking the ice for people to come after. But I'm big and strong and my husband likes it, so I guess we'll get along here all right."

Finding I was from Iowa, she told me there were lots of Iowa people here—more than from any other state.

The dinner went right to the spot. I had two eggs, a glass of milk, bread and strawberry preserves.

I took a look at the place. There was a nice new roomy barn, a water storage system, and a nice garden. She told me that they had cleared about three acres and had planted about an acre of apples, mostly Winesaps. Altogether this was the most inviting farm house I saw in the valley over two miles from town.

Thanking this woman, I wended my way through the sage brush, reached the sand road, and plodded on. Then in the midst of the sage brush I came upon a fairly decent field of alfalfa. A young fellow was irrigating it. He told me he was from the Yakima fruit district in Washington and had just come out last fall with his father. I noticed he was irrigating the alfalfa by the furrow method. In the banks of the little field were the lath boxes every five or six feet. Each box supplied water to three furrows; the furrows were every two feet down the slope of the field. The furrow system for alfalfa was new to me, so I asked the young fellow about it.

"Well," he said, "you see me and pa's irrigated a long

time up in Yakima and have got on to handling this sandy soil. We came down here last fall and everybody was irrigating alfalfa by check plots and flooding. Now, that's all right on fairly heavy soil with a nice even slope and a big head of water. Well, here, like in Yakima, the soil is loose and sandy, there's a big slope, and a small head of water. So we got busy, started using furrows in alfalfa, and now everyone's using it.

"After we planted the alfalfa in the spring we took a marker and marked the furrows down the slope every two feet. No trick at all. Then we turned in the water, and that was all there was to it. You see we have a small head of water for a long time, so we just turn in the water for twenty-four hours or so and it runs down the furrows and seeps across from one to the next."

He had about eight acres. Most of it looked very well. There were some bare spots where it had been blown out and some was short in spots where the soil had been taken off in leveling. The field was cut up into little sections because of the roughness of the ground. The young fellow didn't think so much of the country for alfalfa, but for fruit he thought it should be good, as it was very similar to Yakima.

Then another plod through the sand and I met a man coming down the road in a buggy. He turned out to be an Iowa man looking the country over. He asked me what I thought of it.

"Well," said I, "I don't think much of their wind and sand, but everybody seems to think it will be a great fruit country, so I suppose if a man has time, money, and

Irrigating alfalfa by the furrow method in Oregon (Wallaces' Farmer, *August 27, 1909*)

patience to hang by it for a few years he will make a good thing in the end."

"Well," said he, "that's about the way I size it up. Land's high here, though; but they say it's doubled in value the last two months. I've seen other things looked better to me."

Saying good day, I kept on up the road. The land was all sage brush now, but all subject to irrigation when improved. A mile or so further east I reached the big reservoir which waters the whole project. It has been formed by a dam which has been thrown across a little canyon. The dam is made of earth and faced with native rock. The dam looks solid and big and the reservoir made quite a lake. The capacity is 56,000 acre feet, or enough to cover the whole 22,000 acres of project over two feet deep. A peculiar thing about this reservoir is that it is not filled by the river directly. It is over six miles from the river and

113

filled from the river by a big canal twenty-six miles long. Back up the Umatilla river some eight miles from Hermiston a diversion dam was built to send the water into this long feed canal. When the water is at the flood in the winter the feed canal runs full and the reservoir is filled. The feed canal was built on the high ground straight through and winds in and out following the contour lines. That is the reason it takes twenty-six miles to cover less than ten miles in a straight line.

From the reservoir the water is let into one main canal called the "A" canal. It is so arranged that when the feed canal carries water it can be shot directly into the A canal without going into the reservoir.

From the A canal all the others are taken off. The A canal winds along on the high ground and the canals from it wind along on the high ground below. I followed the A canal for quite a distance. It is on the high ground and I could see the country well. In fact, I could see over three-fourths of the project. The main feature of the view was the rolling, uneven plain dotted thickly with gray-green sage brush. On the far side of the plain were the big hills along the Columbia. Far away to the northeast I could see a big gash between two hills; Columbia gap it is called. Thinly scattered over the sage brush were houses. I could count thirty-seven of them. There were a few spots of cultivated ground. I noticed many clouds of dust sweeping over the plain. Close at hand there was a ditch following around the high ground. After following the A canal some distance I came to where the C canal was branched off. Every canal has its letter and all start from the A canal.

From the A to the C canal was a beautiful piece of

engineering. From the high A line the water was dropped almost straight down a cement ditch to the lower C line. The water slid down this concrete ditch steeper than 45 degrees, I judge, for about 100 feet. It came with terrific force and should be a great source of power.

I followed the C line to Hermiston. The evening was cool and I thought the Umatilla country was pretty nice just because I felt so good in the cool of the evening.

A fine night's sleep and another day at Hermiston. The wind was blowing with great force and a real sand storm was on. The air was gray and the sun was almost hidden by the dust clouds. Out doors it was hard to walk against the wind and the sand ground into clothes and skin. They told me that a sand storm at that time of year was unusual. I stayed out of the storm and spent the day in writing.

The next day I went over to see the very best part of the project. Water was just given last year by the government, so most of the country has had no chance to do much yet. But there is a little that was started by a private canal several years ago. This looks pretty fair. I saw several fields of fairly good alfalfa. There were some nice young orchards and some fine market garden stuff. Strawberries looked especially good to me.

I talked to one man who was from the Wenatchee fruit district of Washington. He thought the country had a good prospect, but that it was a hard fight. He had some very nice young apples and peaches. The apples were Winesaps.

"The common varieties," he said, "are Winesap, Jonathan, and Rome Beauty."

After a little stretch of this alfalfa, fruit, and market garden country sage brush began again.

And that was about all I could see to the Umatilla project—mostly sage brush land, some people working hard to fix it up, a great faith in everyone that it would be a great fruit country pretty quick.

I went out to the government experiment farm. Here I met a bright young fellow from the Oregon Agricultural College. He was conducting the experiments. He was determining the efficiency of rye, field peas, vetch, and barn yard manure to hold the sand from blowing. As soon as he could he was going to plant fruit. He had seen a great deal of the Hood river fruit country and thought this should be good, especially for peaches. To get the land in fruit, he said, first the sage brush must be cleared, then the ground should be carefully leveled, then a holding crop should be put in, and then alfalfa and the fruit. He laid special emphasis on leveling. That was one of the most important points.

I noticed he was using wooden flumes instead of earth ditches. In the sides of the flume were auger holes every four or five feet. These could be closed by a wooden slat. When open the water ran out from the flume and was carried down the furrows. It looked good to me, and he told me that it was more convenient and cheaper in the end than dirt ditches.

He told me, and I had heard it many other places, that the soil changed in composition under irrigation. The seeming sand when irrigated grew heavier and darker in color. The water evidently dissolves soluble matter and disintegrates the sand. The soil is very rich in potash and phosphorus, but is poor in nitrogen and humus, which is remedied by alfalfa.

Irrigation Project at Umatilla, Oregon

There is some desert claim land left yet under the project, but there are men in Hermiston who watch this closely and take up the land when it is thrown open. Nearly everyone in Hermiston seemed to own land. All were very attentive to me and talked the beauty of the country. Some were at the train to see me off. They were such a hospitable people. I was the least bit sorry to leave the country, but I wasn't sorry to move out of the sage brush and sand.

❧ VII ❧

The Boise-Payette Project

In the valleys of the Boise and Payette rivers of Idaho is one of the big irrigation enterprises of the west—about 350,000 acres. This project is interesting because of the climate, crops, and future possibilities, but is especially interesting to us because a large proportion of the farmers on the project are from the corn belt.

At 5 o'clock one morning in late July I stepped off the train at Parma, a little town on the western edge of the project. The town is a typical little country village with a couple of blocks of wooden store buildings facing the railroad track. Finding nothing particularly attractive about the town I left it for the farm of a reader of *Wallaces' Farmer,* Albert Wright, formerly of Warren county, Iowa, who lives a short way out.

As I walked out of town I passed several well kept little places with beautiful little orchards with garden stuff between the rows. Looking over the country generally it looked thickly settled for miles up and down the valley. In every direction were Lombardy poplar trees hedging in the farms. One peculiar thing is the bench formation of the country. First, the valley of the river; then a rise of thirty or forty feet and a long, fairly level stretch of second valley;

Note: Chapter 7, "The Boise-Payette Project," was published in *Wallaces' Farmer,* September 2, 1909.

then above this the foot hills and the mountains in the distance.

The road along which I was walking was good, covered slightly with a yellow dust. One surprise was to see the natural water drainage. I crossed several sloughs with lots of cat-tails or "tulies," as they call them here.

As it should be with a *Wallaces' Farmer* reader, affairs are evidently prospering with Mr. Wright. I met him in the midst of a beautifully level alfalfa field well over knee-high and good for close to two tons of hay on the second cutting.

"We have got a good water right here," said Mr. Wright. "The water is managed by a private concern. It is taken out of the north side of the Boise river up above and brought down here by gravity. There is always enough water except in the months of July and August, when we may have to rotate; that is, one man will take all the water of a lateral and when he is through pass it on down to the next man on the lateral. In this way each man gets the benefit of a full head of water for a short time. Ordinarily the laterals are running full all the time and each man can irrigate when he wants to. On this eighty here I have sixty inches."

An inch, or miner's inch, is a term used for measuring water. Fifty inches in Idaho makes a second-foot. The second-foot and the miner's inch are the two terms of water measurement. They don't mean much unless you know what they will do and how much land they will irrigate, and then they mean a whole lot. Sixty inches on eighty acres, or three-fourths of an inch to the acre, is a good supply of water. Down in Arizona they are satisfied with one-half inch to the acre.

"The government is going to help us out a little with storage water when it completes its works. This will give us plenty of water all the time. As it is we have plenty except occasionally in the late summer."

Mr. Wright started on a discussion of crops. If I hadn't know him for a straightforward man and a canny Scotchman, I might have been taken back at his figures.

"Why," he said, "out of this little town of Parma was shipped $500,000 worth of our products last year."

Then he gave me a list of their shipments:

90	cars of fruit
45	cars of hogs
25	cars of cattle
25	cars of beets
60	cars of grain
10	cars of horses
6	cars of honey
15	cars of seed
25	cars of sheep.

"You notice," he said, "that we didn't ship any alfalfa hay. That is because we have a great sheep feeding industry here in the winter time. Along in the late summer the sheep men contract for our hay at around $5 a ton. Then in the winter they bring their sheep down from the hills where they have been pastured all summer and winter them on our hay in the valley. Last winter there were 250,000 sheep fed here in the vicinity of Parma, and they used 25,000 tons of our alfalfa hay."

Not satisfied with merely telling me the beauties of the country, he took me out to see for myself, saying:

"You can't appreciate what crops we get here till you

see some of them for yourself. I have tried telling our Iowa people back home about them but they can't believe all I tell them. They must come out and see for themselves."

We drove out toward the foothills in the less settled country. The road was good, but fairly dusty. Occasionally we would strike a chuck hole. Instead of mud ruts they have ruts brought about by the continued dryness.

We came to a splendid wheat field, better than any which I had ever seen in Iowa. My friend stopped and we investigated. The wheat reached nearly to the shoulder and the heads were beautifully filled with a large white grain. The stand was nearly perfect and the field spread away beautifully level and uniform.

"Ought to go fifty bushels to the acre and may be more," remarked my friend. "It is on alfalfa ground, and wheat put in right and irrigated right on alfalfa ground ought to give forty to sixty bushels to the acre. We can beat Iowa raising anything except corn."

"We usually sow our wheat along in March. After we drill in the grain we use a 'marker' to furrow the field so as to irrigate it. The 'marker' makes furrows about five inches wide and three inches deep every eighteen inches all over the field. The furrows run from the ditches down the slope. When we want to irrigate we raise the level of the water in the ditch by putting more boards in the check gates. Some people have lath boxes every four or five feet. Then when the level of the water raises it will flow out of these lath boxes in the side of the ditch and down the furrows. Most people dig a hole in the side of the ditch and run the water along a furrow alongside the ditch. From this furrow the water flows down the little furrows across

Wheat stacks, Idaho (Idaho State Historical Society; photograph by Clarence Bisbee)

the field. Every 125 feet or so, depending on the fall, there must be a check box in the ditch. With these check boxes we can back up the water to flow down any certain part of the field. It takes about twenty to twenty-four hours to give a good irrigation. It doesn't take long to learn how to irrigate. A corn belt man can pick it up easily if he keeps his wits about him and his eyes open."

As we drove on we passed a home every quarter or half a mile. The country seemed thickly settled, but the houses were many of them small and unpainted. It is still a new country, but most of the land is fenced. We passed field after field of beautifully level alfalfa nearly hip-high and ready for the second cutting.

"We get six to ten tons to the acre a year from a good alfalfa field. Here alfalfa can be planted in the fall or spring.

Threshing wheat (Idaho State Historical Society; photograph by Clarence Bisbee)

After drilling in the seed we furrow the ground with the 'marker.' Alfalfa takes about six irrigations a year. We harvest three crops."

Almost all the grain and alfalfa fields were in good shape, but here and there were a few ragged and uneven fields, mostly on account of irregular irrigation; the land was not level and the water didn't reach all parts alike.

"One of the most important things in irrigation," said Mr. Wright, "is to have your land level with a uniform slope. The man who starts to farm when his land isn't leveled right runs up against all kinds of trouble."

Then we drove past a blue grass and white clover pasture. I was astonished, for blue grass pastures are not common in the west. It was in fine condition, green and with a nice growth of grass, making a strong contrast to our short, dry pastures of late July and August. On this pasture were ten head of native horses and twelve head of cattle besides some colts and calves. This stuff had been there all season on the fifteen-acre pasture. A head and a half to the acre makes pasturing mighty profitable. In England such land is worth $300 to $400 an acre.

Then we came to a red clover meadow, not common in an alfalfa country. The meadow was a beauty, with clover knee-high and a great abundance of red blossoms.

"We raise great clover seed here, often eight to ten bushels to the acre," commented my friend. "You know back in Iowa we sometimes cut for two bushels to the acre. This is a great seed country. Alfalfa runs up as high as ten bushels to the acre. You ought to see our oats here. They yield around seventy-five bushels to the acre, and are so plump and nice that they weigh forty pounds to the bushel."

After a time we drove past an apple orchard. The trees were about ten years old and the cultivation was just fairly clean between the rows. I looked closely as we drove past and could see only two or three apples.

"Not making much money there this year," I remarked.

"No," my friend replied. "We had a heavy freeze this spring, the worst in history, and practically all the fruit in the northwest was destroyed. But you should have seen that orchard last year. They cleared $1,000 an acre from it last season. They are Ben Davis. Each tree averaged about twenty boxes, and the boxes netted around $1. Our favorite varieties are the Jonathan, Rome Beauty, Delicious, and Winesap. The Ben Davis here is a lot better than the eastern Ben Davis.

"Fruit growing is going to be a great thing in the valley. There are bad freezes once in awhile, but in the good years

124

we make enough to more than make up for the bad ones. I am setting out fruit on a small scale right along."

Then I asked him, "If an Iowa man came out here with $2,000, could he made a go of it?"

"Yes, he could," my friend replied; "that is, if he was the right sort of a man. But he would have to have grit and be willing to work. The best way for him to do would be to buy eighty acres of sage brush land. He would have to go in debt on this, but it would be pretty safe. Good, level, unimproved sage brush land under government ditch but with water right yet to pay for would cost $40 to $50 an acre. Our man would have to clear the sage brush off at an outside cost of $5 an acre. Then he would have to level the ground and put in the irrigation ditches. The crops for him to put in would be grain, alfalfa, and fruit. Grain the first few years would keep him going, then alfalfa, which is the backbone of the country, would fertilize the ground, then gradually getting the land into fruit would make the big money. The first year or so our man would do well to break even, but after that he ought to make good money and pull out all right."

Granting that our imaginary Iowa man was a "sticker" and had his share of good luck, I could readily see how he might make a good thing; but there are many slips possible in a new country which might upset the whole system. Of course there are instances of men who came into the country with next to nothing who bought sage brush land on credit, cleared it, put in crops, and sold it, making several thousand dollars. These men not only have been "pluggers" but they have had good fortune on their side.

My friend drove back home for dinner. While he was

feeding the horses I got a chance to ask his wife what she thought of the country.

"Well, you know Albert likes it mighty well, and where the men folks are satisfied the women folks are pretty well satisfied, too. But this is a whole lot better country for men than for women. We don't have the conveniences here that we had back in Iowa, but I like it a lot better now than when we first came here. It's such a dusty country, too, and that gets on a woman's nerves till she finds out that it isn't dirty dirt like back in Iowa. Then there are dust storms when the dirt sifts into the house in all the crooks and crannies. Last year I had the table laid for threshers. I had called the men in and had gone into the kitchen to bring in part of the dinner. When I came back the plates had a fine covering of dust. It made me nervous; but the men didn't seem to mind it.

"But most of the women here like it pretty well. One lady across the river came here for her lungs. The climate made her well, and she thinks southern Idaho is just about right. There's another lady lives right here next door and she doesn't like it a little bit. But then she hasn't been here but a little while. Her husband thinks the country is just right, and she doesn't let him know what she thinks about it. She will get over it after awhile; some people are homesick wherever they go."

Mr. Wright has four boys of school age who like Idaho just as well or a little better than Iowa. School days they like it a lot better. They are attending a central school near town, and both they and their parents think a lot more of it than the school they had been attending back in Iowa.

Roswell, Idaho

After dinner my friend took me for a drive over the Roswell country, which is supposed to be one of the prettiest districts in southern Idaho. We drove across the Boise river, from which comes all the water for the irrigation of this part of the country. On either side of the Boise river is a valley, a large part of which has gone to alkali for lack of drainage. The main growth on this alkali bottom is salt grass, a short, wiry grass of but little account. Originally this bottom soil was as good or better than any. It was the first land irrigated and produced good crops, but after irrigation had gone on on the higher bench land the surplus water came down carrying the soluble alkali salts. This land won't be worth much until it is thoroughly tile drained.

On some of the higher land in the valley were a couple of corn fields good for forty bushels per acre. Then came the higher first bench land. It was a beautiful country with its broad, level alfalfa fields dotted with the stacks made from the first cutting. Rain is so rare in the summer time that the stacks are left open from one cutting to the next. The first cutting had gone a little under two tons to the acre. The second cutting was just about ready and looked good for close to two tons. The Idaho alfalfa fields are as fine as I have seen anywhere.

Alternating with the alfalfa fields were grain fields and occasionally orchards. The grain, mostly wheat, was just ready for the binder, and looking fine. It is a peculiar thing about this soil, and, in fact, nearly all new arid western soils, that they raise such fine crops of grain and seed where moisture is supplied. This is because the soil is so rich in mineral matter. The soluble mineral plant food has never been washed out by rain or taken away by cropping. There is, however, a shortage of nitrogen and humus; but when this is made up by growing alfalfa the soil will raise phenomenal small grain crops, far superior to what we find in the corn belt.

We drove on up past the first bench to a second bench eighty or one hundred feet higher. From the edge of the second bench there is a wonderfully beautiful view of the pretty farming country known as Roswell. Below us spread the green valley for miles and miles along the river till it lost itself in the distance and flattened against the mountains beyond. Right below us was a checkerboard of alfalfa fields, grain fields, and orchards. Just at our feet one alfalfa field after another ran into the next to form one big plot of alfalfa a quarter of a mile wide and nearly two miles long. The grain fields spread out as thickly covered with shocks as I have ever seen. Close at hand was a dark green square of prune trees. Almost everywhere separating one farm from the next were rows of Lombardy poplar trees. With their branches pointing stiffly upward they give the country rather the appearance of a formal landscape.

The pretty view delighted us for some time. Then, turning away from it, we drove over the second bench. The scene was changed. Instead of alfalfa, grain, and fruit was sage brush, sage brush, sage brush, spreading away mile after mile till the foothills commenced and ran into the mountains. Water makes the difference, and private enterprise couldn't put water on this second bench, but the bed of the high government canal is running over the highest of this second bench land. Water isn't running yet, but it soon will be. When water comes, the change from a sage brush desert to grain, alfalfa, and fruit will be rapid. In prospect of the change there are little unpainted shacks scattered over the plain. The people in these shacks are hanging on until water comes.

Turning around, we drove back into the pretty valley. In driving one noticeable thing was the absence of our ordinary flies, but their places were taken by a half dozen big black flies, half or three-quarters of an inch long. When we got into the valley we raised some fierce mosquitoes. It seems as if any country which will raise good crops will raise good mosquitoes too.

We were back from our drive at 8 o'clock. It was still broad daylight, and stayed light enough to read till nearly 9 o'clock. The latter part of the afternoon and early evening seems the hottest part of the day. When darkness comes a rapid cooling off takes place and the nights are usually fairly cool; a little too cool for the best corn.

Boise, Idaho

The next morning I went east fifty miles on the Oregon Short Line to Boise, the capital and largest city of Idaho. The Short Line crosses the center of the project from end to end, from Parma, on the west edge, to Boise, on the east edge. From the train I could see the same crops everywhere—grain, alfalfa, and fruit. Not all of it was good. In fact, there were a good many ragged spots in the grain fields along the river bottom land. The railroad follows the Boise river and one does not get the best impression of the country, for it is along the river bottom where the poor drainage and the alkali make the land look bad.

Boise is a pretty little city of close to 25,000. Like all western cities, she has growing pains, and is out with her slogan, "You'll Like Boise Best." Boise is nice, with plenty of trees, clean streets, and pretty homes. Although on the eastern edge of the irrigation project, she is making herself the commercial center by running out interurbans to the west. At present there are two lines running, and more being constructed. I took one of these interurbans and ran out west of Boise about fifteen miles. Close to town the interurban ran through some very orderly, well kept little truck gardens. The Chinese do most of this work. Further out were several cleanly cultivated orchards. Then came the grain and alfalfa land. Every mile there is a station. At several of the stations I noticed milk cans standing. At nearly every station farmers were getting on and off. The line seemed to be doing an active business among the farmers. The homes along the line were for the most part cleanly kept little places and attractive. At one little station about fifteen miles out I stopped off.

I had walked a mile or so along a very dusty road between fine grain and alfalfa fields when I saw a man, shovel in hand, irrigating a rather poor oat field. I stopped to talk, and found that the oats had been sowed late and that there had been a shortage of water a little earlier in the season when they should have been irrigated. Furthermore, the land was not level so the water could be put on evenly, and for all these reasons the oats were looking ragged. The young man was using a sort of flooding system in his irrigation. I wanted to see how he worked it, so I got a pair of overalls, a shovel, and took off my shoes; he had a pair of rubber boots, but had none extra. It wasn't hard work irrigating by the flooding system, but it was mighty "poky." There was a little ditch made by throwing a plow furrow both ways, coming along the highest ridge of the land. Leading off of this main field ditch were laterals, also on the high ground. It was all the primitive type of irrigation practiced in the valley for years. There were no wooden check gates to back up the water to make it flow down a particular lateral. Instead, we would take dirt from the sides and the bottom of the ditch to make a dirt dam to raise the level of the water. Then where we wanted it to flow out on the land we would dig a hole in the side of the ditch and let the water run. We would fool around a bit, scratching little furrows here and there with the shovel till the water got to spreading smoothly. Then we rested on the handles of our shovels and gossiped till the water had spread far enough, when we would work a few minutes closing up old holes in the side of the ditch and making new ones. The work looks simple, but it takes a man with what they call the "irrigator's eye" to wet some irregularly sloping pieces of ground so that some won't be left dry.

While we leaned on our shovel handles, waiting for water to spread we talked irrigation farming. "Really now," I said, "what do you think of the flooding system of irrigation for grain and alfalfa as compared with the furrow method?"

"Well now, I'll tell you," he said. "Around Boise here they use the flooding system a good bit. It has one advantage that I can see over the furrow method, and that is that when you cut either the alfalfa or grain on furrowed, or corrugated land, as we call it here, the furrows and ridges every eighteen inches shake up a mowing machine and the temper of the man who is riding it. If you are going to use furrows you must level the ground better to start with, but after you have the furrows made it's a whole lot less work to irrigate a piece of ground, and then it gets the water more evenly and the soil doesn't puddle and bake. The state experiment station here recommends using the furrow method with check boxes in the ditches and lath boxes in the sides of the ditches to supply the furrows. That's all right; but there will be a lot of flooding for a long time yet in Idaho. A very few people here on very level land use levees about a foot high every fifty feet. Then they flood in between the levees like they do in California.

"You see that low, marshy land just below here? Well, I bought that at $70 an acre last fall. I have a drain ditch built through it, and as soon as the piece gets drained of the water and the alkali it will be worth $150 to $200 an acre like the rest of the land around here close to the interurban. Before it went alkali it was some of the best land in the valley. You see the people here are pretty careless with their water, and a lot of the bottom land is spoiled by using too much."

"What is your average sized farm here?" I asked.

"Well, most of the farms here close to the interurban are eighties. An eighty in alfalfa and some fruit makes a mighty nice proposition. This is going to be a fine fruit country here some day. We had hard luck here this spring, but we can raise as good fruit here as can be raised anywhere. The trouble now is that we haven't got the fruit spirit in the country yet. We're not like the Hood river country where they raise fruit and nothing but fruit. When we get the fruit spirit here, the intensive cultivation, the spraying, and the co-operative methods of picking and selling, land will take a big jump in value.

"Did you say you was from Iowa? Well, we have lots of Iowa men out here, and we're glad to get them, too, for the corn belt men make as good farmers as we've got; a whole lot better than some of the old-timers who were cattlemen and can't seem to get over the idea. Back in the old days most of our men were Missourians. In the eighties there was an Irishman, a democrat, in the valley by the name of Governor Stuart (he had run for governor once). Whenever he met a new man he would say, 'Well, what part of Missouri did you say you was from?' In the late eighties President Harrison was out in Idaho and Governor Stuart was introduced to him as one of the prominent men of the neighborhood. The governor shook hands, and then inquired after his usual manner. 'Well, what part of Missouri did you say you hailed from?"

I had what I wanted of irrigation by flooding, so I struck for the interurban, and was soon back at Boise. The next morning I met Mr. Hanna, the project engineer, who was going out to inspect the Deer Flat reservoir, and asked me to go along. We drove across from Caldwell. Caldwell is a thriving little town which has dreams of surpassing Nampa and Boise. Out of Caldwell was the same beautiful grain, alfalfa, and fruit country. This country is watered by a private company, the Pioneer Irrigation Company. In fact, practically all the older developed country is reached by private companies. The government is not going to buy out these companies, but is going to help them out with storage water when they need it for a certain price, not yet determined. It is going to be somewhat difficult to tell just how much of a water right there is on some of this land. In Idaho there is no law as yet making the water right a part of the land, to be sold with it, that is, appurtenant. It is to be hoped that the government will soon get all this land under private companies straightened around so that the amount of water right may be easily determined.

As we drove Mr. Hanna outlined the project to me. The whole Payette-Boise project will water about 350,000 acres. All the water is to come from the Boise and Payette rivers. During the months of July and August the river will not flow enough for all the land so storage must be practiced. Most of the work so far has been done on the land south of the Boise river. A diversion dam costing a quarter of a million dollars has been built across the Boise river seven miles above Boise City. This dam diverts the water from the Boise river into the main south side canal. This canal follows the high ground, and after winding for thirty miles empties into the Deer Flat reservoir. Besides feeding the reservoir the main canal gives off laterals to water the country in between. This main canal cost three-quarters of a million dollars. The government has nearly completed the work on the south side of the river, and will soon be ready to furnish water to the 130,000 acres under this part of the project. The work on the north side of the river is just being started. To water this part right reservoirs must be made up in the mountains where the Boise river rises. On the Payette river a diversion dam is to be built and a storage reservoir is to be made of the Payette lakes. The government will do well if the total cost of all this work runs under $10,000,000.

After driving several miles through the developed irrigated district we came to the sage brush. The road got dustier; the horses pushed along through a fine, yellow, fluffy powder covering the road four or five inches deep. The trotting of the horses and the turning of the wheels raised the dust in quantities and the wind threw it back in our faces. It filled every pore of the skin, made our eyes smart, and in our mouths we could taste it and feel it gritting against our teeth. Now I could see why people who drive much across the sage brush wear linen dusters and sometimes goggles.

At last we came in sight of the upper dam of the Deer Flat reservoir. It was simply a big wall of dirt thrown for more than half a mile across a big opening in the hills. It contains, so Mr. Hanna told me, almost exactly a million yards of material. We drove across on top of the dam and looked over the reservoir. It was nearly empty, but when it is filled it will hold 136,000 acre-feet of water. This is figured to be enough storage water for 120,000 acres. The reservoir appeared to be just a big depression between the hills. Naturally there were two big openings in the hills. The government has just got these two openings closed by two big earthen dams. After three or four miles of driving through the hot, dusty sage brush we reached the lower dam. This dam is close to two miles long, but it contains a million yards of dirt, the same as the upper one. The two cost something over $6,000,000.

As we drove back across the sage brush I asked Mr.

Hanna how he thought an Iowa man could do if he came to Idaho to buy a farm with $2,000. Mr. Hanna wasn't very optimistic about the imaginary man's chances. In fact, he seemed to think that, unless the man was a hard worker and had plenty of good luck, he would make a failure of it.

Back in Boise, I met Mr. Hubbard, an old Iowa man, who is a great enthusiast over Idaho, and particularly over the new sage brush land which the government is getting ready to water. He took me out about ten miles through some beautiful orchard and alfalfa country to the little town of Meridian. There we took a team to drive south to the sage brush land. The land just south of Meridian is under what is called the Ridenbaugh ditch. A little over a month before I saw the land the Ridenbaugh ditch, which runs for a ways on a side hill, had broken and before the water could be turned off the water had washed a big hole in the side hill. The wash was filled and a flume was put in, but the work had been done hastily and the break occurred again. The result of all this trouble was that the farms under the Ridenbaugh ditch below the break were dry and had been dry for a month before I saw the country. Pastures were dry and looked much like our pastures in August after we have been without rain for a month. Alfalfa and trees were just commencing to suffer. Of course, when the farmers found that they were without water in a country where it rarely rains from May till October a great clamor went up. When drouth occurs in the rain country we feel that it is a matter of Providence and we can fold our hands and grin and bear it, but these poor farmers when they saw their crops burning up for lack of water which could easily be had if the ditch were only fixed were mightily disposed to raise a big outcry.

Then we got into the sage brush country and the same thick dust came up which I had met the day before. The country is fairly level and the sage brush spread away gray-green and gently rolling for mile after mile. This land sells at $40 to $50 an acre with absolutely no improvements and no water right. The government will soon have water ready for this land and the water right can be bought from the government according to the terms of the reclamation act. As soon as the government works are completed the actual cost of them will be charged to the land benefited and each acre will have to pay its proportionate share. No interest is charged and the money due may be paid in ten equal annual installments. This sage brush land will have to pay about $40 an acre, or $4 a year for ten years, to the government for its water right. Then before this sage brush land can produce anything it must be cleared of sage brush, leveled, and plowed. Ditches must be laid out and a crop planted.

I said to Mr. Hubbard, "It must be a hard pull to get this land into shape to grow crops and make money."

"Well," said Mr. Hubbard, "It's not as hard work as you would think. Now it was only five or six years back that all that pretty grain and alfalfa land this side of Meridian was in sage brush. It isn't much trouble to clear the land of sage brush. The old-fashioned way was to grub it out with a mattock, and that cost close to $5 an acre. Now the commonest way is to take a couple of railroad irons sixteen feet long, bolt them together, and draw them over the sage brush with four horses. After the sage brush has been dragged twice with this most of the brush is loose and can be raked up and burned. It costs about $3 an acre to clear land of brush with a railroad iron. A third way is to use a sort of an A-shaped machine with saw teeth along the edges of the A. This cuts the sage brush off below the ground, and is said to do fine work.

"Leveling is more expensive, varying in cost from $5 to $15 per acre, depending on the unevenness of the ground. It is very important after the brush is off to level the ground well so that the water will spread evenly. Then the ditches must be put in, the ground must be plowed deep, and you are all ready to put in a crop."

"Now, Mr. Hubbard," I said, "if an Iowa farmer came out here with $2,000 could he succeed?"

"Yes," said Mr. Hubbard, "I believe he ought. He should buy forty acres of sage brush land under the government ditch at $50 an acre. He could get this by paying a fourth or half down. Now, the way I would have this man work his farm would be to put ten acres as soon as possible into pasture grasses—blue grass, orchard grass, timothy, white clover, alsike clover, and red clover. We have the finest pastures here on earth. Another fourth of his land he should put into alfalfa; another fourth into grain to keep him going at the start; and the last fourth he should get into fruit. Now this man wouldn't have any easy time of it at first; it takes a worker to make a success of farming anywhere."

The sage brush we were driving through was tall, rank stuff, three feet high, but occasionally there were little spots ten feet or so square where the sage brush was stunted. These are "adobe spots," which are caused by the extreme stiffness of the soil. Adobe soil is just as rich as any other but it has a bad reputation, for it won't grow much until the stiffness has been taken out by continued cultivation. It is like our clay, but worse. It seems as though soil everywhere has something which you must be on your guard against. On the lower bottom soils you must watch for alkali. On the higher bench lands there is lots of stubborn adobe, and on any of the soils you must be sure that you have a good water right.

We drove over a sage brush rise called Orchard ridge. It seems that speculators have bought this from the home-steaders and are selling it out in ten-acre lands for fruit farms. It ought to be good fruit land, for it is higher than the surrounding country and should be less liable to frost. I would not like to live on ten acres of this sage brush land while my fruit trees were coming into bearing.

All this desolate looking sage brush land which is to come under the government project has been filed upon and there are little, unpainted homestead shacks scattered thinly over the entire tract. Water has just started to come this year and not much has been done, but next year when the water comes regularly a great change should take place.

Mr. Hubbard is president of the State Dairy Association and is very enthusiastic over dairy prospects in southern Idaho. As Mr. Hubbard sees it, the climate, feed, and market are ideal for the dairyman. The summers are much the same as ours; but drier, and the nights are cooler; but the great advantage of the Idaho summer to the dairy cow is the almost entire absence of flies. The winters are short and moderate, zero rarely being reached. For this reason the cows may be left out doors during a large part of the winter. Pastures are an easy proposition for the Boise valley man. Under irrigation blue grass is green and may be pastured almost any month in the year. It is figured that an irrigated blue grass pasture should carry at least a cow and a half to the acre. For feed about all that is needed is alfalfa hay, which can be produced on the farm at a cost of $2 a ton. The market is excellent: Idaho has been importing butter. This last summer the price for creamery butter has been running about 35 cents. Mr. Hubbard gave several instances of men who had done splendidly. One man had a cream check of $92 for one month from eleven cows which had been pastured on five and one-half acres. The favorite breed in the valley is Holsteins. Dairying is no doubt quite profitable, but it is doubtful if many farmers will start "pulling teats" until they are compelled to in order to make money.

Mr. Hubbard showed me some wheat that had been put in this spring on sage brush ground. It looked a lot different from the magnificent fields which I had seen on alfalfa ground. The stand was not as even, the straw was shorter, and the heads were not as well filled. To bring any arid western soil up to its full producing power alfalfa must be grown to add nitrogen and humus to the soil.

As we were driving back I asked Mr. Hubbard: "How does this Boise valley country compare with the Twin Falls country we hear so much about?"

"Well," said Mr. Hubbard, "the Boise valley has several big advantages; it's lower in altitude, being only about 2,800 feet while the Twin Falls country is over 4,000, and consequently there is a greater liability of frost in the Twin Falls country; there is a much greater wind velocity in the Twin Falls country, which makes the dust storms a much more disagreeable proposition. Then the Twin Falls country is all watered by Carey act companies and we don't believe that they can do as satisfactory work as can the government.[1] Of course all the Twin Falls projects are newer and land can be bought cheaper."

The next day I went down to Nampa, took a wheel and rode out to the northwest of Nampa. All this country is higher bench land well back from the Boise river. Just within the last few years it has been taken from sage brush and put into cultivation. As I rode along on the wheel the country looked much the same to me as the lower more developed bench land, but the grain fields were not as even in stand and the alfalfa was a little shorter. I stopped to talk with a man who was getting his derrick ready to handle his second cutting of alfalfa. He was from the Palouse wheat country of Washington and was "sore" as could be on the Idaho country.

"This is no country around here to make money," he said. "It's a good place for the easterners to come out here and get fooled on the fruit land. This land, half of it, is dobied and you can't raise much of anything on it. Those real estate men say you can get six to ten tons of alfalfa to the acre, but we're only getting three tons around here and we've only been getting $4.50 and $5.00 a ton for it, so you can see there isn't much money in raising alfalfa. There's a sugar factory down here at Nampa, but the beets around here this year are almost too poor to use. Give me the Palouse country; I can raise wheat there without much work in the rain country and make money."

[1] For an explanation of the Carey Act, see page 158.

I rode on some distance and saw a man shocking oats. I said to him: "Your neighbor down here from Washington doesn't seem to think much of this part of the country."

"No, he don't, but it's his own fault; and he's a nice fellow too. You see he came here, rented his place down the road there, and the real estate men soaked him on the rent. Then he didn't know anything about irrigation, so he's been sore on the whole country.

"Yes, there's lots of adobe on the land through here, but adobe is not bad after once you learn how to handle it. Now this oats here that I'm handling ought to go forty or fifty bushels to the acre, and it's on the worst dobied land in the country. All it takes is careful working. We use corrugations or furrows on this adobe soil. You see, if you flood adobe it bakes, so we level the ground off and put in the corrugations every eighteen inches."

I rode on further and saw them plowing land that had just been cleared of sage brush. I got off my wheel, and as I walked across this land I could see the spots of stiff adobe and lighter, fluffier soil alternating. The adobe was cloddy and I could walk on the plowed adobe without sinking, but on the sandier soil I would sink nearly to my ankles. The adobe is richer in plant food, but it won't raise nearly as much at first as the lighter soil. I saw a big cloud of dust in the distance and, just making out the outlines of a team, I supposed that someone was harrowing.

At the next house I stopped was a family of Missourians. The house was just a shack and the lady of the house, who was getting along in years, was quite disgusted with the lack of conveniences and the dustiness of the country.

"Yes," she said, "this may be all right for young people

to come out here and fight the sage brush, but it's pretty hard on the old folks. I'd be pretty glad to get back to Missouri. I don't believe the people out here are as hard workers as they are in the corn states. If they were they'd make a lot more money than they do. The sun is so hot here that I don't blame them for not working hard."

That afternoon I rode back over the dusty roads to Nampa and caught the train for Minidoka. The Boise country impressed me as quite a place for the young man to come and make his way by farming and living on the land. It may make a great fruit country. If so, land will increase greatly in value. At any rate, the valley should be a great alfalfa, grain, dairying, and feeding country on an intensive scale.

❧ VIII ❧

The Minidoka Country of Idaho

In southern Idaho in the valley of the Snake river from Minidoka to Buhl are some of the largest and most interesting irrigation enterprises to be found in the world. Including both the government and the Carey act projects there are over a million and a half acres which are to be irrigated. This makes the largest tract of irrigated land in the world. Of course most of this great area will be handled by private corporations under the Carey act, but the government has a large and interesting enterprise in the Minidoka project.

I stopped off at Rupert, the government headquarters of the Minidoka project, about 10 o'clock one morning in early August. Rupert is a government townsite, and shows the effects of it, for it is one of the most dilapidated little towns which I have ever seen. All the buildings are little square frame affairs with just enough ambition to be painted. The ramshackle buildings are arranged on four sides of a square which has a fine stand of blue grass and white clover which the town hasn't had energy enough to mow. There are a few poplar and locust trees which may make some shade some day. I made my way to the bank, a one-story frame building about fifteen feet square. Here I met Mr. John McQuiston, an old Des Moines man who

Note: Chapter 8, "The Minidoka Country of Idaho," was published in *Wallaces' Farmer,* September 24, 1909.

144

is out in the Idaho country for his wife's health. He explained to me the reason for the town's shabby appearance.

"As you know," he said, "this is a government townsite and when people first started coming in here four or five years ago they just squatted on the government land on the townsite and built any sort of an old shack in which to do business. Later the government held an auction, and now most of the land is in private ownership. It's going to take us some time to get rid of these old frame buildings, but we're starting to put up some substantial brick buildings this year."

Mr. McQuiston took me on a drive to a forty of his of which he is very proud. As we drove I noticed two things particularly: The ground is very level, spreading away with hardly a dip or a rise as far as I could see; and the soil is very sandy. When the buggy wheels would roll through the sand of the road they would make a noise very much like that which a heavy wagon makes when it creaks over the packed snow at 10 degrees below zero. Mr. McQuiston is homesteaded on his forty acres; he has only forty acres because that is the farm unit one and one-half miles from town. All the rest of the farm units are eighty acres, and as practically all the land in the entire 120,000 acres of the project has been homesteaded on, it means that this tract will have a far denser population than the average Iowa farm community.

We got out of the buggy and examined the wheat field, which had a splendid stand. The straw stood nearly shoulder-high and the heads were long and well filled. Mr. McQuiston estimated fifty bushels to the acre for the field. He considers himself very fortunate; his farm is "subbing"

Rupert, Idaho (Idaho State Historical Society; # 70-1836)

(getting the moisture by sub-irrigation), so he doesn't have to irrigate. All he has to do to keep his crops supplied with water is to keep his field ditches filled with water. The water sinks into the sandy subsoil and rises to the surface of the field. There were two fields of wheat; one sub-irrigated while the other had been surface irrigated; the sub-irrigated field had a much evener stand and better filled heads. His sub-irrigated potato field showed up as prettily as any potato field which I have seen anywhere; no weeds anywhere and a fine sand mulch over the whole field. I dug down a couple of inches and struck the sub-irrigation moisture coming up from below, then a couple of inches more and I struck a large potato which the moist sand fell away from leaving it clean and white and free from scab. Then he showed me his alfalfa field planted last spring. It stood over knee-high and good for close to two tons to the acre on the second cutting; it had gone almost two tons on the first. There were two fields of young alfalfa sown this spring; one field had been surface irrigated and seemed to have a fine stand of strong plants ten to twelve inches high; the other field had been sub-irrigated and didn't show such an even stand or so strong a growth. It seems that though some crops thrive better on sub-irrigation alfalfa and fruit trees object, and demand surface irrigation to do their best work. Moreover, if sub-irrigation is carried on long in a country the water table rises and alfalfa and fruit trees are forced to retire, as neither of them like wet feet.

This is only the third year that irrigation of any sort has been carried on in the project, and this spring the eastern part of the project with the more sandy soil started in "subbing." All those who own farms which are now "subbing" regard themselves as in luck. They look on sub-irrigation as a blessing which renders surface irrigation no longer necessary. I hardly blame them for their rejoicing, for standing around irrigating with a shovel as most farmers do is "poky" business at best; but sub-irrigation is not an unmixed blessing. The trouble is that it can not be controlled; ground which is subbing beautifully one year may be a marsh the next, at least such is the experience of farmers in the older irrigated districts. In a level sub-irrigated country drainage must go hand in hand with irrigation.

That afternoon I walked out west of town to see the country and find the sentiment of the people regarding it. The first man I met was a Missourian who was living in the ordinary little, unpainted homestead shack. He was mightily pleased with the country, for his place had started in subbing this spring. He had ten acres of beautiful young apple trees with potatoes between the rows, all without a weed.

I walked on a bit farther to the next shack, where I found a Missouri woman at home. Her opinion of the country ran as follows:

"No sir; I don't think much of this country; it's too dusty and the sand storms are something awful. There aren't any trees yet and the sun comes straight down and scorches you. It may be all right here for a young man to make his way, but for an old woman like me Missouri is a lot nicer."

At the next shack a woman from the Sacramento valley of California was at home.

"No," she said, "I don't like this as well as the Sacramento valley; the winters are too cold; it sometimes gets down a little below zero. Then we don't have any fruit here yet. But I don't mind the dust as much as most of these people. We'll drive to town and get our clothes blown full of dust and then when we come back all we have to do is to hang our skirts out on the line and let the same wind which blew the dust in blow it out again. No, it's not so very lonesome; there are people on every eighty and within a mile and a half of town on every forty. And they're nice people too, and they don't spat the way they do back in the country I came from.

"We've homesteaded on this forty about three years, but we'd sell the relinquishment for $2,000. Three years ago it was all in sage brush, but now it's all cleared and some is in alfalfa."

I trudged on down the heavy sand road, passing some excellent alfalfa irrigated by the furrow method. The oat and wheat fields were most of them rather uneven and of poor stand, due, I suppose, to the fact that the ground had not yet been enriched by growing alfalfa and also the people are new to irrigation and haven't leveled the ground right to spread the water evenly.

Then I came to a shack in which an Iowa woman was at home. She had come out into the country originally for her boy's lungs but although her boy's lungs had improved she found the altitude, the sunshine, and the dust storms hard on her nerves.

"Yes, we've found it a pretty hard life in this country, but we've lived three years on this homestead and we're going to stick till the finish. The worst is past now; at first we didn't get water when the government promised it to us, then when we did get water the wind was so strong that we could hardly get anything seeded down before the wind would come along and blow it out or cut it down. There's one good thing, we don't have any electric storms here like we used to back in Iowa. I just got a letter the other day from back home saying that lightning had killed two people and set a barn on fire. We have things fixed pretty nice here now. There's a nice clover and alfalfa meadow over to the north of the barn."

The clover was fine, as good as the best in Iowa, and much thicker with blossoms than any Iowa clover. I commenced to take some stock in the tales they tell of six to ten bushels of clover seed to the acre. The alfalfa was knee-high and just ready to cut. One novel thing about both these fields was the fact that the levee or check system was being used. The fields had been perfectly leveled and levees had been put up every fifty or sixty feet. It struck me that the check system should be good on nearly all of the Minidoka land; it is so level naturally.

As I walked west the soil became much more of a clay and sub-irrigation stopped. It seemed that the soil was not porous enough to permit of it. I met a man irrigating potatoes; the potatoes were up on rather high ridges with deep furrows between and the water was flowing down the furrows. I asked the man why they used such deep furrows.

"Well," he said, "that's to keep our potatoes from getting wet. If the furrows weren't so deep the water would come up higher and get the tubers wet and that would make them badly shaped. As it is, the water just comes high enough for the fine feeding roots to get it. We can raise the finest potatoes on earth on some of our soil. This here is a little bit too clayey to raise the prettiest potatoes."

The next man I met was a Georgian, and although pretty badly discouraged, he was going to stick by his homestead another year and prove up on it.

"The wind plays _____ here; we no sooner get the land cleared of sage brush and something seeded when along comes a big sand storm and cuts it all out. I tell you it makes a man feel pretty sober when he gets a nice stand of alfalfa started and then a wind comes and cuts it down before his eyes; and after he's done this three or four times he feels pretty sick of the country. But thank goodness those days are nearly past; in a few more years we'll have this country pretty well down to alfalfa, and we'll get trees started, and then this ought to be a mighty nice country to live in."

The next man was from Montana. His sentiments ran something like this:

"I have been on this homestead three years and I'm going to stick by it two more years till I can prove up on it; no relinquishing for me. This spring the wind blew my grain out and some of my alfalfa, but I don't think it will be so bad in another year. You know they tell the story here of a man who planted [a] garden on one side of the tract but the wind picked it up and blew it fiftcen milcs to a man across the river on the other side of the tract and he raised the garden.

"These people around here are not a very high class of irrigators. I came from a part of Montana where they know a little bit about good irrigating. There's one thing these people have to learn, and that's to level their land carefully before they put in their crops. When the government opened up this country for homesteading just about five years ago it brought in a rather poor class of people. They came here without money and for the first two years had an awful hard time hanging on, for the water wasn't ready yet and on their own places there wasn't anything but sage brush for them to live on, so a lot of them went to work for the government on the ditches; then when the water did come they didn't have enough money to fix their land right, and they just stuck in their crops haphazard.

"Yes, there's a lot of discouraged people from whom you can buy relinquishments anywhere from $400 to $4,000 for an eighty, but I'm going to stick."

Buying a relinquishment is merely buying the right to homestead on a certain piece of land instead of the man who was formerly homesteading. The man who buys the relinquishment presents the relinquishing papers at the land office together with his filing on the land. Then he goes on the land as though it had never been homesteaded; he must live on it five years, put one-half the land under cultivation, and pay all charges of the reclamation act before he can receive the patent to the land.

The further west I went from town more of the land was still in sage brush, but here out about five miles I struck an excellent eighty acres owned by an Iowa man. Twenty acres had an excellent stand of young alfalfa; ten acres were irrigated by the furrow system and ten acres by the check or levee system. The furrow alfalfa had ranker growth, which may have been due to the fact that the ground hadn't been carefully leveled for good work under the check system.

"What will you sell your relinquishment for," I asked.

"Well," he said, "in another month I can prove up and then I'm going to sell the whole eighty for $4,000. We want to get out of here; the altitude and the sun and the dust is hard on my wife's nerves. It oughtn't to be such hard work this next five years, but it was a long, hard pull at first here."

The next day McQuiston, Jr., drove me up to the big government diversion dam in the Snake river, twelve miles above Rupert. By this dam is diverted all the water which is used on the 120,000 acres under the project. For two miles to the northeast of Rupert the land is in a pretty fair state of cultivation. There is some fine alfalfa, some fair grain, and some healthy young orchards.

"Say, McQuiston," I said, "what sort of a fruit country do you think this will make?"

"We think it's going to be a great fruit country. Of course we haven't had water here long enough yet to bring any orchards into bearing, but over here in the hills in some of the mountain canyons and of some of the earlier private irrigated places there has been some fine fruit raised. We set out over a thousand fruit trees on the tract this spring."

As we drove further northeast from town the alfalfa and grain fields became less frequent; practically all the land is yet in sage brush, but every half mile or so is the ordinary little, unpainted homestead shanty.

Some of the land is too rough for cultivation; there are big chunks of lava scattered over it. Most of the way up to the dam we drove along the bank of the main north side canal. As we drove I could not but be impressed with the excellence of the government's work. The banks of the canal are strong and smooth; wherever a lateral is taken out a concrete headgate is put in; all the bridges over the canal are built with concrete piers.

Then we came in sight of the big lake backed up in the Snake river by the Minidoka diversion dam. The lake is over a mile wide and backs up the river for nearly twenty miles. Of course the size of the lake has no effect on the irrigation, as this dam acts merely for diversion and power and not for storage. Standing on the edge of the lake I could see the big concrete headgates on both the north

153

and south sides of the river into which the water is diverted by the dam for the two big main canals. The dam is a tremendous affair. First on the north side comes the power part of the dam. This is built of concrete and has seven big ten-foot openings for the water to rush through and operate turbines. Only one of these openings is now connected with a turbine. After the water goes through the turbine it falls down into the main north side canal and is just as good for irrigation as though it had not had the power taken out of it. The main part of the dam is 600 feet long, built of earth, with lava rock facing and a cement core. Then to the south of the main dam comes the prettiest part of the whole thing, the 3,200 feet of spillway. This is where all the Snake river which is not used for irrigation by the Minidoka project goes over. The face of this spillway is concrete and the water describes a beautiful parabola in

Diversion canal and gate, Minidoka Dam (Idaho State Historical Society)

going over. The cost of the dam was a little over half a million dollars.

Besides this diversion dam the government is building a storage dam up on the head waters of the Snake which will make a reservoir of 800,000 acre feet. This storage water, together with the natural flow of the Snake, will give the Minidoka project one of the best water rights in the country. On the river the government has second priority rights, the South Side Twin Falls people having first. As the Snake is one of the big rivers of the west, there is small likelihood of its failure, but if it should, the Minidoka project will be nicely fixed with a tremendous storage reservoir. The entire cost of the government works in the end will be about two and a half million dollars. The government has already fixed the cost of water right to the people at $22 an acre, and it now looks as though the government were going to come out in the hole. At $22 an acre the Minidoka project is one of the cheapest and best watered projects which the government is behind. As with all government water, the $22 may be paid in ten annual payments without interest. The annual maintenance charge is about 60 cents an acre.

The dam is not entirely completed yet, and there is a big crew of men working on the cement power house. McQuiston knew them all. I wondered, and asked him about it.

"Oh," he said, "all those fellows are ranchmen (in the west all farmers are ranchmen) here on the project. You see they haven't been able to get enough to live off of their places yet, so they come and work for the government on the ditches. That's the trouble in a newly homesteaded country; the people don't have any money to make improvements and the country moves slowly. Few men with money want to tie themselves down to a country for five years. That's the difference between this and the Twin Falls country; the people down there have money; the country has been cleared faster; and land values are higher, although land is worth really no more."

After looking over the dam we drove down below a half mile to get ferried over to the south side of the river. The ferry is a big scow attached to a cable, the current pushing the boat across the river. The south side of the river is one broad, level sage brush plain from the river to the mountains. The notable feature of the south side is the pumping system; 50,000 acres are to be irrigated by pumping. The main south side canal goes as far as it can by gravity, but there is a lot of good land higher up further away from the river which should produce fine crops if it only had the water. To get the water on this land pumps are used. There are three series of pumps, called the first, second, and third lifts. When the gravity system has gone as far as it will the first lift raises the water thirty feet, and then when this has gone as far as it will another lift of thirty feet is made, and then another.

We stopped at the first lift and the attendant explained some of the workings. Electric power comes over the high tension line from the power dam and is transformed at the lift and made to work a big centrifugal pump which throws the water up a big four-foot pipe into the upper canal thirty feet higher. We climbed to the upper canal and then looked down thirty feet and saw the water below us; that impressed us.

The next morning I left for Twin Falls. As an absolutely

reliable proposition I was much impressed by the government project at Minidoka, but it is a backward country, the people are without money, and there is no booming whatever. It should grow steadily, however, and a thickly populated little farming country should develop here. The government has done a great work by creating homes for 5,000 people where there were none before. The Twin Falls country is forty miles below Minidoka, and in climate and soil is much the same as the government project; but in the methods of development it is entirely different. All the Twin Falls irrigation has been done under the Carey act. I will tell something of it next week as it impressed me.

The Twin Falls Project of Southern Idaho

The Carey act, passed by congress in 1894, is one of the greatest land acts ever passed. It authorizes the secretary of interior to grant to each of ten of the arid states of the west arid land up to a limit of a million acres on condition that the states would irrigate it and sell it to actual settlers. The land thus obtained by the states is usually irrigated by private irrigation companies under the supervision of the state engineer and the state land board. Before any of the land is open to filing the state engineer must certify that there will be plenty of water for irrigation in the district set apart for that particular company to water. Filings under the Carey act are made on 160 acres or less. Fifty cents is paid to the state for the land, one-half down at the time of entry. The big expense comes when the private company is paid for watering the land. This varies from $13 to $60 an acre and may be paid in ten annual payments with accrued interest at 6 per cent. Under a Carey act project the entryman buys his land from the state and his water right from the irrigation company. The entryman must begin living on his land within six months of the time the company puts water on it. Then to get a title all that is necessary is to build a house on the land, cultivate an

Note: Chapter 9, "The Twin Falls Project of Southern Idaho," was published in *Wallaces' Farmer,* October 1, 1909.

eighth of it, and live on it for thirty consecutive days. Of course this means that Carey act land changes hands a lot more than homestead land, for it is a simple matter to prove up on Carey act land and sell at an advance. The method fosters a certain amount of speculation but it booms the country and makes it grow.

The Twin Falls country presents an entirely different appearance from Minidoka country. The South Side Twin Falls project under the Carey act and the Minidoka project under the reclamation act started about the same time but the Twin Falls project is years in advance of the Minidoka project merely because it has had more advertising, more booming, and has attracted a more progressive class of people.

The success of the original South Side Twin Falls Carey act project has attracted a lot of capital into the irrigation construction business and there are now completed or in the course of construction the following projects in the vicinity of Twin Falls; (1) South Side Twin Falls, 240,000 acres; (2) North Side Twin Falls, 180,000 acres; (3) Clover Creek, 45,000 acres; (4) Bruneau Extension, 600,000 acres; (5) Salmon River, 140,000 acres; (6) Goose Creek, 52,000 acres; (7) Dietrich, 50,000 acres; (8) Idaho Irrigation, 150,000 acres; (9) West End Twin Falls, 50,000 acres; (10) King Hill, 15,000 acres; (11) Bruneau, 150,000 acres. The first four tracts get or will get their water from the Snake river; the rest will get their water from the storage of flood water of creeks over the country. Not all of these projects which are now being constructed have been approved by the state engineer under their present acreage and water supply. On the Snake river the South Side Twin Falls tract has first rights, then comes the government project at Minidoka, and the other projects must come after these two have plenty of water.

The South Side Twin Falls tract is the only one which shows much development past the sage brush stage. I stopped off at Twin Falls, the famous little five-year-old city of southern Idaho. From a sage brush plain to an up-to-date city of 5,000 in five years is rapid development. From sage brush land worth 50 cents an acre before water came a city has been developed worth, according to the assessment valuation, $1,500,000. I couldn't help but be impressed by Twin Falls with her five or six blocks of substantial brick store buildings and a couple of fancy hotels which would be a credit to any city in Iowa.

I took a drive out southwest of Twin Falls toward the Sucker Flat country, so called because it was originally settled by Illinoisans. The first man at whose place I stopped was an old Nebraska man. He had come into the country six years ago with just $5 to his name. He worked on the ditches for the company and earned enough to file on forty acres of land and meet the first payment. The land then was all in sage brush, but he hired a team, and working with it cleared ten acres; five acres he put in potatoes and five acres he put in oats seeded to alfalfa. From the potatoes he cleared enough to buy a $250 team. Ever since then he has been making money. His land is worth $200 an acre, partly because it is within a mile of Twin Falls.

"What are your big paying crops here?" I asked him.

"Our best crops," he said, "are going to be alfalfa, sugar beets, and winter apples. We get six or seven tons of alfalfa to the acre and $5 a ton for it; and all the time we're

160

building up our soil. The alfalfa makes this quite a winter sheep feeding headquarters. I have never raised any sugar beets, but the experts say this is fine soil for them, and some of the neighbors have been getting around fifteen and twenty tons to the acre. There's no factory here yet, but there ought to be one pretty soon. I believe this is going to be a great winter apple country; on one old irrigated ranch near here they made $1,000 net per acre. The favorite varieties are Jonathan and Rome Beauty."

"How about your irrigation company here," I asked, "is it giving you good satisfaction?"

"Well, there's one thing I can say about it: They're giving us all the water we can use; but they'd play smart with us if it wasn't for our canal union. You see, the law provides that the company at the end of five years can turn the system over to the farmers. Well, the company here wanted to turn it over; but they hadn't done their work right and the canal union got out an injunction against it. You see, the company had put in a lot of wooden headgates where the contract called for concrete, and the company wanted to turn over the works with the wooden headgates, which would have increased the maintenance expenses 'to beat the band.' "

"I don't understand what made your farmers here co-operate and work together on the matter. Our farmers back in Iowa and Nebraska wouldn't do it."

"It's just a case of have to; that's all. If we didn't co-operate we couldn't do a thing with the company. Then irrigation naturally makes a closer union among the farmers; farms are closer together and the farmers have to combine to divide the water among themselves."

As I drove on past this farmer's place I was favorably impressed with the country. There were broad, level fields of rank growing alfalfa; wheat and oat fields had an even stand with rank straw and well filled heads; young orchards were healthy and fairly well cultivated. The country I was driving over differs from the Minidoka country in that it is rolling and the soil is less of a sand and more of a clay. I was driving along a good road, but with the usual thick yellow dust.

The next man I met was an old Des Moines blacksmith. He came here four years ago when the country was all sage brush and Twin Falls just a dot of shacks on the sage brush plain. Now he has fifty acres of alfalfa, some mixed pasture, and some sugar beets. He is one of those men who enjoy scrapping; he has a law suit against the water company, and you don't have to stir very deeply to find out his sentiments about the company.

"My neighbors all say, 'Sh! don't knock on the country,' but I think there's some things here that ought to be talked about. This irrigation company has to be watched all the time or it will turn over the works to the farmers before they're done and concrete headgates are put in. I don't think much of these Carey act propositions; they look to me like tremendous grafts. They're all right if the state engineer and the state land board are only straight, but it's my private opinion that they're only human and are influenced tremendously by the irrigation companies.

"Then I think a lot of these real estate men around here are grafters, too. They say you can clear sage brush land for $3 an acre, plow it for $2, and level it for from $5 to $10. Now it's my experience that these figures are all low;

$5 an acre at least should be allowed for clearing, $3 for plowing, and $10 up, according to the lay of the land, for leveling. Then they say their wheat here averages from forty to sixty bushels to the acre; I estimate the average to be twenty-five bushels to the acre. On old alfalfa ground, though, the average will run forty bushels."

This man took me out and showed me his alfalfa and his system of irrigating. The alfalfa was splendid, nearly hip-high and good for two tons to the acre at the second cutting. Along the upper side of the field a ditch was running with check gates every 135 feet or so. In the side of the ditch every ten feet were wooden boxes with openings about two inches square for the water to run out of. The inside opening of the box was provided with a wooden slide to control the amount of the water let out on the field through the boxes. Each box watered eight or ten furrows. The furrows were eighteen inches apart, five inches wide, and nearly five inches deep. All this made the watering of the alfalfa very simple. Put the splash boards in a check gate so that the level of the water will raise and the water will flow out the boxes and down the furrows through the field.

As this man expressed it, "there's not much to irrigation if the ground is leveled right to start with and the ditches are run right. With ground fixed like this an Iowa man can soon learn how to irrigate as well as anyone."

With all his pessimism this man said, "I wouldn't change this farm for two Iowa farms. This is going to be a splendid winter apple country and fine for dairying and sheep feeding. I don't think much of so much grain raising; in the future I believe that most of the land will be in fruit and

Irrigation in Idaho (Idaho State Historical Society; photograph by Clarence Bisbee)

alfalfa with the alfalfa used for feeding dairy cows and sheep."

The next place at which I stopped was a dairy. A woman owned it, and with her hired hands, was just starting in to milk her forty cows. The cows were mostly grades with a few pure Holsteins, but most of them were strong in their udder development. The owner said she was making good money; butter fat was selling for 28 cents a pound. The cows were being pastured on an irrigated pasture of blue grass, orchard grass, meadow fescue, and white clover. Their only additional feed the year round was alfalfa hay. As there is no fly season, the cows keep up nearly as strongly in their milk during July and August as during any other season of the year.

Then I came to the edge of the famous Sucker Flat

The Thomas Woods ranch, Twin Falls, Idaho (Idaho State Historical Society; photograph by Clarence Bisbee)

country. Here magnificent shoulder-high grain fields alternate with splendid alfalfa; the yellow grain and the green alfalfa roll off for a long way toward the west, making it as pretty a farming country as one could ever wish to see. I stopped at one farm and learned that the land was selling at from $75 to $100 an acre.

One thing I noticed very generally on the South Side tract was the poor water. Ditch water is used almost altogether for domestic purposes; it is filtered from the ditch into the cistern. Most of it is quite yellow in color, and I fancy it could furnish a large number of bacteria to the drop.

After looking over the developed South Side tract I went down to look over one of the new tracts, which is going to be opened this fall. I rode for nearly thirty miles on

165

horseback across that tract and practically all I saw was sage brush. Sage brush rolls away gray-green for mile after mile, and that is all there is to the tract. And with water that is all there needs to be, for the ordinary sage brush ground with water produces wonderful crops. I knew that if this dry, desolate, gray looking sage brush land got plenty of water there is no reason why it shouldn't be as pretty a farming country as the South Side tract. There are a great many thousands of acres of sage brush land which companies are planning on developing whose success depends merely on the abundance of the water supply. Some of these companies will get their water from the Snake river and others will get it by storing up creeks at the time of flood. In all cases there will be a somewhat less certain supply than on the developed South Side tract which has first right on the river. Under the supervision of the state engineer and the state land board these companies are supposed to be able to sell only as much land as they have plenty of water for. If these state officials are infallible and unprejudiced in their judgment of water supply, these projected tracts should be perfectly safe.

The Carey Act

The working of the Carey act is very interesting. Some men praise it to the skies; others dam it utterly. As one gentleman high in the reclamation service pointed out to me, a Carey act company usually clears a half to a million dollars of clear "velvet." This is charged to the people. Some say that the Carey act projects are cheaper than the government projects, but they are not; a $30 to the acre Carey act project, with its accrued interest at 6 per cent, is actually more expensive at the end of ten years than the $35 government project. And the work isn't nearly as good; naturally a private company puts as little money as it can in the works and then when the works are shifted to the people they will have a tremendous maintenance expense on their hands keeping faulty works in shape. The influence big companies can bring to bear on state land boards must be terrific, and it would be quite wonderful if a large amount of faulty construction did not find its way into the works of many of these Carey act projects.

On the other hand, I found many people who were great admirers of the Carey act system as it had worked out. As they see it, a country develops much faster under the Carey act than it does under the reclamation service. Carey act lands are more advertised, more people come in, and land values rise more quickly. Then a private company can do things which the government can't on account of red tape. For this reason a Carey act project is usually completed more quickly than a government project started at the same time. The Carey act companies often have a higher class of engineers than the government, for the simple reason that the government pays rather low salaries and Carey act companies can and are stealing government engineers by offering advance in pay.

The government reclamation service undoubtedly puts in more substantial works, and does it at cost, without interest. Of course the government may work slowly, make some bad blunders, and not advertise the project much. But the growth under a government project should be strong, healthy, and sure, and in my estimation, more to be preferred in the end than the growth under a Carey act

project with a less sure foundation. Readers of *Wallaces'*
Farmer are advised to investigate most thoroughly before
buying Carey act land, and make sure that the construction
is good and the water supply abundant. Land in this country
without water is worth little more than the state sells it
for—fifty cents an acre.

❧ X ❧

The Grand Valley and the Greeley District of Colorado

Four hundred miles west of Denver on the west slope of the Rockies is the famous Grand Valley of Colorado. As a fruit country it is one of the most favorably known valleys of the world. It is different from most valleys; more like a hole in the ground with the sides running straight up; and the sun beats in and reflects from the steep sides or palisades to make the fruit color and flavor beautifully.

I stopped a day to see this wonderful country. I was fortunate in running across a gentleman who is thoroughly well informed concerning the valley, and I said to him: "I wish you would tell me something about the disadvantages here; I will hear enough of the advantages before I get away."

He hesitated somewhat, but finally started in to criticize the Grand Valley for me:

"Our greatest trouble here is late frosts in the spring. A year ago last spring we were caught worse by frost than at any other time in the history of the valley. The blossoms came out beautifully and the whole valley was a mass of bloom when a late frost came, and as a result there was almost an entire failure in the whole valley. A few growers used coal and crude oil smudge pots, and the way the

Note: Chapter 10, "The Grand Valley and the Greeley District of Colorado," was published in *Wallaces' Farmer,* October 8, 1909.

orchards of these few men bore was a lesson to the whole valley; so this year when the frost came around again at blossoming time we were prepared for it and the result is that this season Grand Junction has one of the best fruit crops in the entire country.

"Besides frost there is another big enemy, the codling moth, which makes us spray all our fruit with great care. In such a district as this where everyone is growing fruit there are bound to be a good many insect enemies, but we are keeping them down pretty well by spraying.

"Then there's another thing, and that is the adobe spots, like the soil close around town here, which won't grow anything well at first and which isn't the best fruit soil at any time. There's some seepage, as there is bound to be in any irrigated district."

"So, as you see it," I said, "the main disadvantages of the country are late frosts in the spring, codling moth, and adobe spots? But there is another thing I would like to ask you about, and that's the price of land. I hear a bearing orchard sells for from $1,500 to $4,000 an acre. It looks to me as if a man would be 'going some' to make money on land with it at such prices."

"Well," said he slowly, "I don't know but it is a little bit high. Of course there have been years when market prices and yields were just right when tremendous profits have been made, profits as high as $1,000 an acre. On the basis of such profits land has been sold for $2,000 to $4,000 an acre, but I believe that's high, for one year with another a fruit orchard won't produce such tremendous profits; there is too much danger of early frost and insect enemies."

The state experiment station has a branch here and I

hunted up Mr. Weldon, the horticulturist. He had a big array of smudge pots which had been used with success during the past spring. Several types had been invented in the valley, which shows what a live question smudging is. There are two types of smudge pots; one burns coal and the other crude oil. In the spring when frost is threatening the pots are set filled with fuel between the rows of the blossoming trees. If any night looks dangerous the whole valley is awake ready to light the pots if need be. The heat generated by the pots is enough to raise the temperature four or five degrees, which will often make the entire difference between failure and success in the fruit crop.

In talking with Mr. Weldon he assured me that there were a lot of good things about the country which he hadn't time to tell, and that the disadvantages of which I had been told were controllable.

One of the very interesting features of the Grand Valley is the fruit growers' association, which differs in many respects from any other association of its kind. I had a talk with Mr. Jones, an officer of the Grand Junction Fruit Growers' Association. He gave side lights on the secrets of the success of the organization in a few short sentences.

"Farmers always deceive themselves as to the quality of their products. We grade so closely that every buyer knows that the grades of fruit which we put on the market are exactly as they are represented to be and consequently is willing to pay full price without making any allowance for poor quality. That's one reason for our success; we keep our grades exactly up to standard. Another reason is that we allow the growers as much leeway as possible and yet keep the quality of their fruit up to standard. The growers market through us, for they all have confidence that their fruit will bring the full average price of the market. One item of success is the close touch which we keep on the market through the men who handle our fruit at the big markets. We have the right of diversion from the railroads, and when we see that a given car has been billed to a glutted point we divert to a stronger market. From time to time we issue publications advising our growers how to handle their fruit. For instance, here is a sheet just issued to our growers advising them concerning the picking and packing of Bartlett pears. All our growers do their own picking and packing; we merely do the grading, shipping, and marketing. For doing this we charge a 5 per cent commission, but as all the stock of the association is owned by the growers and one grower can not own more than $1,500 worth, any dividends resulting return to the growers. During the slack season in the winter time we do a merchandise business to keep our force busy. We have been handling confectionery, soap, twine, and various articles of necessity in the valley, and by means of this side business have been enabled to return quite a dividend, as high as 20 per cent."

The organization of the association is simple; there is $100,000 worth of stock, owned entirely by the growers, the limit for one man's holding being $1,500. The stockholders meet once a year, at which time they elect a board of seven directors which gets together once a month and appoints the manager and other employees of the association. For manager a high class man is needed, as is evidenced by the $5,000 a year salary which is paid. The simplicity of this organization gives the actual gowers and packers direct control over all important movements through their representatives, the board of directors. During the twelve years of its organization the association has made tremendous growth, till it now handles a million dollars' worth of business, which makes it one of the big cooperative associations of the country.

On the next day was to come the big Iowa picnic. Posters were out announcing the fact, and excitement was in the air. Although I didn't have time to stop over for it, I benefited by it. Lieutenant Governor Clark of Iowa was at Grand Junction as the guest of honor the next day, and I went for an automobile ride with the lieutenant governor and Mr. Auperlee, an old Iowa man but a long time resident of the valley. For a short distance out of the town of Grand Junction the land was largely bare on account of the adobe. We drove up on a hill at the side of the valley and looked down at the level stretch of green fruit trees spreading for miles and miles up and down the valley. Six miles across the valley the palisades stuck straight up into the air and then merged into the mountains, which went up higher yet. Then driving down into the valley proper we went for many miles through the fruit belt proper. There were nothing but orchard trees on either side of the road; mostly peaches, pears, and apples. All the trees were beautifully healthy, but best of all they were loaded with fruit till they could hold no more. On many of them, Mr. Auperlee said, the fruit had been thinned once, but still the trees were producing heavily enough so that some exceptional trees would produce as much in money as an acre back in the corn belt. In between the trees cultivation was perfect; not a weed anywhere. Every three or four hundred yards the trees would stand back for just enough space for a neat little house. I was struck with the average beauty of the houses and the frequency with which they were scattered along the road. The average size fruit farm is ten to twenty acres, which makes the entire valley almost one village and, indeed, the farmers on the fruit ranches do have a large share of city advantages with mail, grocery, and ice delivery; centralized schools; and in some cases electric lights on their porches. The road over which we were smoothly rolling was slightly dusty, but otherwise in beautiful condition. The day was very warm, but it seemed cool in the shade of the fruit trees.

As we passed one beautiful place Mr. Auperlee told us a bit of the history to illustrate the wonderful development in the valley. A horticulturist by the name of Smith, washed out by the Galveston flood, came to Grand Junction and entered into a five-year agreement with a Mr. Dudley to care for one-half the crop for a forty-acre orchard which the latter had bought for $4,000. Soon afterward Dudley got a chance to sell the orchard for $10,000; Smith refused to give up his contract, but himself offered $10,000 in four annual payments. During his first four years of management Smith cleared $5,000 each year, and at the end of four years owned the farm, besides having made a good living. A little over a year ago Smith sold the farm for $48,000. Mr. Auperlee told us a great many similar stories: this place had just sold for $4,000 an acre, that one had just returned a net profit of over $700 an acre, etc., etc. These are of course extreme cases.

We hardly knew when we got to the town of Palisades; the houses were a little closer together and there were a few stores, but the fruit trees continued right up into the town. Mr. Auperlee took us into a fruit shipping house at Palisades where they were grading early peaches. After tasting a good many samples of the peaches we were even more in love with Grand Valley.

Turning around, we sailed once more down the thickly populated little valley with its rows and rows of heavily loaded fruit trees. Every house had in front of it a sign with the name of the ranch, the owner's name, and a blackboard on which was chalked up any fruit for local sale. For instance: "THE GOLDEN WEST RANCH, Peter Jackson, Owner. For Sale: Two bushels Bartlett pears; four spring chickens."

Of course all the orchards are irrigated, the water coming from the Grand river in private ditches. Mr. Auperlee assured me that the Grand furnished an abundant water supply; in fact, that there is enough water for a great many more acres than the 25,000 acres now set out to fruit. For several years he had been trying to interest the government in irrigating a large amount of land which without water is worthless but with water soon becomes the most valuable farming land in the United States. Prospects are favorable now for the government to start a reclamation act project.

Mr. Auperlee told one story to illustrate the quality of the Grand Valley apple: A Colorado man took some Grand Valley apples to a convention of French horticulturists at Paris. The apples appeared so perfect that the Frenchmen thought that they were wax until they were cut into and each man was shown a sample. Then they claimed that the fruit had been artificially flavored, and were not convinced that apples could grow so perfectly till they had been analyzed chemically.

In the cool of the evening as we were coming back from our wonderful drive Governor Clark remarked to Mr. Auperlee: "The drive this afternoon through your wonderful valley has been worth all of the long trip out here from Iowa."

As I reviewed the Grand Valley I was forcibly impressed with two things: First, the wonderful beauty and productiveness of its orchards, and secondly, with the heat of the sun beating into the hole in the mountains. Farming is under ideal conditions from the social point of view when ten acres will support a family. But the high price of land, the late spring frosts, and insect pests all combined to offset these attractions to a certain extent.

The next morning I came east from the Grand Valley on the Denver & Rio Grande. For fifteen or twenty miles the track ran between the orchard trees, but then suddenly the valley narrowed; close on one side of the track was the Grand river and on the other side rose the mountain wall straight up; no room here for orchards. The memory of the valley remained all the sweeter on account of the sudden contrast with the barren rocks. For several hundred miles now the track lay over the Rocky Mountains, with but very little chance for farming of any sort. Creeping close beside the river with the mountain wall rising sheer on the other side, the track led up and up till finally just before reaching Leadville the divide was passed and the track shot down from an altitude of over 10,000 feet to 7,000 and 6,000 feet and followed the canyon of the Arkansas instead of the Grand. Then the Royal Gorge of the Arkansas with its sides running sheer up and up for half a mile. Then passing Colorado Springs, the famous

pleasure resort, and Denver, the progressive mile-high city
at the base of the foothills, I came in northeastern Colorado
to that famous center of irrigated potato growing, Greeley.

Greeley, Colorado

As I found the town of Greeley in my short visit it is a
bustling, clean little place of about 9,000 people. Greeley
was founded nearly forty years ago and named for that
famous New York newspaper editor who fathered the
saying, "Go west, young man, and grow up with the
country." The Greeley district is one of the old irrigated
sections of the country. Wishing to find out what the
people thought of the country I struck out from Greeley
on foot. As I went north I crossed a little river, the Cache
La Poudre, from which comes the water for irrigation
either by direct diversion from the river or by storage. To
my right I noticed a big sugar beet factory. The land along
the river ran in a level bottom land for a quarter of a mile
or so and then rose to a first bench. The bottom land being
close to town, it is largely in garden truck. Seeing a man
irrigating cabbages, I stopped to see how he did it. He was
using sewage from the town, and as it came down the ditch
at the upper side of the field he dammed it up and caused
it to run down the furrows between the rows, flooding
seven or eight rows at a time. The man was leaning on his
shovel watching the water run and had plenty of time to
talk. The bottom land along the river, he told me, is very
rich soil and on account of its closeness to town is worth
$300 and $400 an acre, although in the spring it is often
badly flooded by the Cache Le Poudre. A bit further on
came a rise in the land and the first bench commenced. I

177

walked through a beet field of eight or ten acres which was in excellent shape with fine stand and very smooth, evenly shaped beets. Then I came to a disgraceful looking alfalfa field; in fact, I must say that all the alfalfa fields which I saw in this neighborhood were rather poor. The alfalfa was just starting after the second cutting and was having a hard fight against the grasshoppers. There were no furrows down the field to assist in irrigation; irrigation is evidently done by flooding. The ditch on the upper side of the field was cleanly dug and free from weeds, but there were no wooden check gates to back the water up for flooding. From what I saw of the alfalfa around Greeley I was disappointed; it seemed short and lacking in vigor compared with the Idaho alfalfa.

A little further on I came to a potato field worth seeing. The field spread out from the road for half a mile; the rows went down straight as a die; not a weed could I see, and the potatoes were still green, healthy, and growing, not withered and dead as our Iowa potatoes become from the attacks of blight before they are three-fourths grown. A bit further on a man was irrigating his potatoes, and from what I could see of it, it didn't appeal to me as being especially good for one of the older irrigated sections of the country. As the water came down the field ditch at the upper side of the field he dammed it up with an earthen dam which he had made with his shovel, and then cutting a hole in the side of the ditch above the dam, diverted the water into a little ditch which ran parallel to the main ditch. From this little ditch he diverted the water down the furrows between the rows. These furrows ran straight as a die; they were very deep, the water when running down them not coming high enough to wet the young potatoe tubers. As the man worked with his shovel, now throwing a shovelful here and now a shovelful there, and meanwhile resting on his shovel handle, it struck me as a "puttery" sort of job at best.

I asked this man: "How many bushels do you think you're going to get an acre?"

"Well, this is a pretty fair field and it ought to run about 175 sacks (about two bushels to the sack). A sack brings anywhere from 80 cents to $1.60. One fellow down the road here sold $9,000 worth of potatoes off from eighty acres." The price is not always so high. Not many years ago they sold one season for 35 cents.

A bit further on they were threshing oats. A young fellow here had some time off and told me something of the crops of the valley. Potatoes are the big crop of the valley, from which most of the money is made. Sugar beets are also a money-making crop, but take lots of help. Both sugar beets and potatoes take fertility from the soil. To build this fertility up again alfalfa must be grown, and alfalfa is grown more as a fertilizer than as a forage crop, although three cuttings may be cut, running as high as five tons to the acre, selling for $7 or $8 a ton. The place of the small grains is mainly as a nurse crop for the alfalfa to keep the weeds down; although the grains do very well. In this particular oat field, which this young man was helping thresh, the yield was estimated at seventy bushels running forty pounds to the bushel. This field, like many others over the valley, was a disappointment, owing to the fact that the stand of alfalfa with the grain had been destroyed by the grasshoppers.

179

As I walked on I was favorably impressed by the good roads spreading on level, smooth, and fairly free from dust. One either side are rows of big spreading poplar trees. Another very noticeable point is the beautiful homes; the houses are more substantial, better painted, with better kept yards than any other general farming district in which I have ever been. The valley seemed very beautiful with its fine houses, good roads, and some trees, spreading away quite level and quite far in the distance up rose the mountains. Quite a common thing in connection with many of the farms is a potato cellar, a big, compactly built shed, often partly under ground.

I found it hard to understand just how they handled their water rights. As I finally came to see it, water is sold by rights at $3,000 a right, which is supposed to be enough to water eighty acres. Besides this there are reservoir rights which may be bought to help out in case the river right isn't sufficient.

Altogether the Greeley country impressed me as a beautiful section with pretty homes, but with land running at $200 and $250 an acre it hardly seemed a place of tremendous opportunities for making money by farming.

Dry Farming near Cheyenne, Wyoming

From Greeley, Colorado, I went north some sixty miles to Cheyenne, in southeastern Wyoming. It happened to be "Frontier Week" there, an annual event in Cheyenne, and the town was crowded worse than Des Moines is during the Iowa State Fair. Frontier week is a tremendous celebration, the biggest thing of its kind in the country. People gather at Cheyenne from a half dozen different states, and the week is spent in stunts peculiar to the west—roping contests, wild horse racing, broncho riding of the most terrific sort, etc. Some horses after successfully throwing all would-be riders for several years establish most evil reputations, and people come from great distances to see such horses ridden. One horse called "Steamboat" is known throughout the northwest, and while I was in Cheyenne the air was full of speculation as to whether he would be successfully ridden this year. Last year he was ridden for the only time, but it was muddy at the time and it was considered that the horse did not have a fair show. As my time in Cheyenne was limited, and I was more interested in seeing something of the agriculture there, I did not wait to see whether Steamboat sustained the record he had built up.

Note: Chapter 11 on dry farming near Cheyenne, Wyoming, was published in *Wallaces' Farmer,* November 26, 1909.

At Cheyenne I met Dr. V. T. Cook, one of the most enthusiastic dry farmers in the west. In fact, he believes it possible to raise crops under the dry farming system where the annual rainfall is as little as 8 inches, but he says to do this a reservoir must be made of the ground and two years' moisture must be stored up for one big crop. Dr. Cook's system is about the same as Mr. Campbell's. To make a reservoir which will retain the moisture efficiently the plowing must be deep, 8 or 9 inches. The western soil is very hard and compact and the water will run off the sod without soaking in; but after it has been plowed deep it is like a sponge and will absorb 20 per cent of its weight in moisture. The best time to do the plowing is in the fall, so that during the winter the soil may have a chance to take up any moisture that falls. It is not best to harrow after fall plowing because this is more likely to cause the soil to blow during the dry winter season; but after all spring or summer plowing the ground should be harrowed at once and a dust mulch made, which is necessary in retaining the moisture. The ground which is being summer fallowed to gather the moisture for the next year's crops must be harrowed or disked after every rain, to break any crust which would allow the water to evaporate rapidly.

Under dry farming conditions much less seed is used than in the humid sections: for example, they use only 30 to 40 pounds of wheat to the acre. This should be drilled in with a press drill and the seed put next to the moisture; but to start the seed successfully the moisture must be close enough to the surface so that the three conditions necessary to germinate and grow seed are present—moisture, heat, and oxygen. I heard of a crop of wheat being lost on one of the western experimental dry farms because of putting the wheat in too deep in the anxiety to reach moisture. An important process with winter grain crops is spring cultivation with a harrow or weeder to put on a good dust mulch and thus keep in the moisture. This must be done when the ground is in just the right condition. Otherwise the crop will be injured.

In many of his ideas Dr. Cook differs with Mr. Campbell. The latter believes that the subsoil packer, an instrument used to pack the subsoil, is necessary for the best dry farming. Dr. Cook seems inclined to hold that under Wyoming conditions the subsoil packer is not needed so much as Mr. Campbell seems to think. Dr. Cook evidently believes that Mr. Campbell is overlooking the importance of crop rotation and fertility. Dr. Cook says: "We must rotate to supply the humus which is necessary to enable the soil to hold water. The ground wears out under dry farming conditions as surely as under any other, and rotation, or fertilizers, must be used in the end to keep up the fertility."

The doctor is a firm believer in the future of the dry farming country of southeastern Wyoming, but he says that a good dry farming system must be followed to raise crops. The ground must be summer fallowed; one-half the ground lies fallow each year while the other half raises a crop. According to the doctor, one man should be able to dry farm 160 acres with but little extra help. He says that the most paying farms will be those on which all the crops are fed to live stock and the manure returned to the soil, thus adding to the humus and increasing the moisture-holding capacity of the soil. The doctor felt that *Wallaces' Farmer* had not given the dry farming country a square deal.

He said that we ought to have a farm in that country to really understand all of the conditions. He holds that dry farming may be successful on 12 inches of rainfall.

Like many other western people, Dr. Cook has evidently formed his impression of how *Wallaces' Farmer* stands not from what *Wallaces' Farmer* or its publishers have said, but from what someone has said that we have said. Land boomers in the west have quite generally circulated stories to the effect that *Wallaces' Farmer* is against dry farming and against the west. All sorts of lies have been told about the paper and its editors. Careful readers of the paper are not deceived by these stories, but many others have been.

I spent a day in the country about thirty miles east of Cheyenne where there has been quite a land boom during the past two or three years. At one of the little towns near I met Mr. Alexander Hastie, an old Des Moines real estate man, and some other Des Moines people. Mr. Hastie took me in his automobile and drove out some three miles to his home that evening.

Parenthetically I might say that it is the custom in this country for real estate men and boomers to meet all trains with automobiles and see that land seekers meet only folks who talk favorably of the country, and so far as possible see only the show farms. Automobiles are used to show the land, and many a man has purchased a farm which he supposed was close to town only to find when he went to drive to it later that it was ten, fifteen, or twenty miles away.

The country there is rolling and very little of it in crops. We passed a fair looking corn field, some rather good wheat and oats, a field of Canadian field peas, and some

184

fair sorghum. Most of the country, however, is still in the native buffalo and grama grasses. Up to a few years back this great prairie with its nutritious grasses was a cattle country; the immense pastures were fenced up. But the cattlemen owned only every other section, the rest being owned by the government. These government sections were of course subject to entry under the homestead law, and settlers moved in here and there. This naturally brought about conflict between cattlemen and the ambitious home-steaders. In some cases where a few sections were home-steaded in large pastures an agreement was made by which the homesteader allowed his cattle to run in the pasture and had the use of the ranchman's bulls. In return for this he fenced his own crops against the ranchman's cattle and looked after the cattle at one or two watering places during the winter. While in many cases the cattlemen and homesteaders got along without trouble in this way, in many other cases there was friction which often developed in bad blood. In 1906 the government took a hand in the matter and compelled the cattlemen to remove their fences which included government land. This, combined with the overwhelming desire for land, has brought about a transformation in all of the cattle country which offers any reasonable prospect of growing crops. The ranches are being broken up and the settlers are coming in with the plow.

I found Mr. Hastie's home on the banks of a creek, the only one in that section of the country, and greatly valued on that account. Along the creek were a few scattering groups of cottonwood trees, the only trees of any size for miles around. The combination of a few trees and a little water is so unusual in that country that it is greatly valued. People in this country come long distances to picnic beside a small pool of water and a few trees. Although the middle of August, the evening was distinctly cool and I had a fine night's sleep. I was not much surprised the next morning when I took a look at Mr. Hastie's corn. It had been well cultivated and was well grown, but the ears did not look very much like the ears we see in the corn belt. The nights are too cool on account of the altitude. It had rained a little on the afternoon of the day before, but this morning the porous red soil had soaked up the moisture and it was dry enough to cultivate. Mr. Hastie took me through quite a good deal of the country in this region. We passed a few fields of wheat and they were mostly good. The stand was a little thin, but the heads were long and well filled with fairly plump grains. Many of the fields had just been cut, and from the thickness of the stubble in the field I judged that the yield should run over twenty bushels in some cases. The roads here are good. Speaking generally of this section, the crops looked very well; but I saw no summer fallowing nor any special effort toward good cultivation to conserve moisture. The average rainfall at Cheyenne, twenty-eight miles away, and the nearest station, for the period from 1871 to 1906 was about 13 inches yearly. When I was in this section, the middle of August, they had had over twelve inches of rainfall in the two-thirds of the year which had passed. The rainfall for four or five years past has been above the average in this region. When it drops as low as ten inches, which has occurred eight times in the past forty years, the folks here must do better farming if they expect to grow anything. At the present time, and evidently for two or three years back, they have been doing about the same kind of farming to which they have been accustomed in the humid regions. This will do fairly well in years of excessive rainfall, but when the dry years come they will have no water stored up in the soil, and crops will be short, if indeed they grow anything. A successful rotation, which should include a legume crop of some sort, must be worked out if agriculture is to be built up here. Alfalfa can probably be grown in spots fairly well if rains come at the right time during the seeding period to give the young plants a start. In the end the permanent success of this and other similar country in the west will depend upon mixed farming with stock raising, both to maintain the fertility and water-holding capacity of the soil and to market crops to the best advantage. Dr. Cook recommends the feeding of lambs, cattle, and hogs of the bacon type on the dry farms.

At its best a dry farming community will be very thinly settled, school houses will be few and social life limited by the distance between the homes. Dry farming is the reverse of irrigation farming in many ways. Much more land is needed for dry farming; prices are much lower per acre; the character of the farming is extensive rather then intensive. I was not able to spend enough time in the dry farming country to write about it as fully as I would like. I was there long enough to learn, however, that this year at least there has been a good deal more dry farming done on paper than in the fields. Comparatively few of the people in eastern Wyoming—at least of the men who are actually living on the farms—seem to have any very practical ideas concerning dry farming. Perhaps one reason is that they

187

have not felt the need of it so much during the past year or two. The real estate man in that country can tell one very much more about dry farming than the farmer can. They talk about it, but they don't do it.

Western Real Estate Men

Speaking of real estate men, the western country is overrun with them, especially the country between Omaha and the Rocky mountains along the main line of the Union Pacific and up both forks of the Platte. An immense acreage of land has been sold during the past two or three years and there has been a good deal of money made, especially by speculators who have bought large tracts and sold it off in small tracts. Some of these real estate men are reliable and some are pastmasters in the art of deception. Some of them have regularly employed cappers at each of the towns from which they show land—men who are farmers or who dress as farmers, and who make it a point to get acquainted with every stranger who comes to town, ascertain whether he is looking for land or not, and if he is, to steer him up against the real estate man for whom he is working. From the time he starts west with a crowd of land seekers until he gets them on the land and sells to them, the real estate man has two main thoughts in mind: One, to keep some other land agent from stealing his customers, and the other, to steal the other fellow's customers if he can. Some of them have an organized system by which men who are supposed to be farmers and land seekers get on the train at different points on the westward journey, get acquainted with the crowd under the real estate man's charge, and join them. These men are the first to buy when the land is reached, and keep the real estate men posted on what each individual thinks, how much money he has, what piece of land he thinks the most of, etc. The man who goes west to buy land should take his time to it. In the irrigated country he should make certain of the water rights, and he should avoid land subject to alkali. In the dry farming country he should stay long enough to get somewhat acquainted with the country and with farmers who have lived there for some time. He should not form his opinion from one or two show places. He should remember that an hour's ride in an automobile means half a day's journey in a light rig and a day's journey with a loaded wagon. And he should not be fooled by stories of increasing rainfall. There is nothing whatever in the records of the United States Weather Bureau to justify the claim that rainfall increases as the plow comes in. There is a variation from year to year, but no permanent change in the average for a period of years.

৯. XII ৯.

Branding on the Alamositas Ranch

It was 4 o'clock one June morning in the north Texas panhandle. I had just stepped off the train, and except for the railroad track not a sign of civilization was in sight. Then a lantern came bobbing through the darkness and the man behind the lantern took my suit case without a word and carrying it a hundred yards placed it in a two-wheeled cart. I climbed in and we drove away through the darkness to the ranch headquarters at Alamositas. The wheels droned along steadily through the sand, breaking the stillness of the early morning. I asked the driver if many people got off at the station.

"Well," he said, "I reckon some one gets off every three or four days, but I don't really know because I'm doing another man's work this morning. He went over to Channing last night to a dance and hasn't got back yet, so I had to come over to meet you."

Conversation lapsed; man's faculties are at a low ebb in the early morning. The sun was just lighting the east when we drove up at ranch headquarters. My driver showed me a room and advised me to lie down a bit. I dozed off, but was awakened in a short time by a voice in the next room.

Note: Chapter 12, "Branding on the Alamositas Ranch," was published in *Wallaces' Farmer,* December 24, 1909.

"Come alive, boys—come alive—come alive. 'Iry'—come alive, Ed—come alive."

This was repeated for about five minutes without variation and I came alive in short order. I went out on the porch of the ranch house and met Mr. Mitchell, the foreman. It was 6 o'clock and day had just broken. Such a clean, far view it was from the porch. For miles and miles I could see across the "breaks." The "breaks" are the rough series of small, choppy hills found in the northern panhandle along the rivers. The "breaks" sloped down gradually for eight or ten miles to the river and then rose for another eight or ten miles on the far side. They looked of a fresh, greenish blue in the cool of the early morning. The world looked bigger and cleaner and fresher than I had ever seen it before.

We went in to breakfast and I met a couple of fourteen-year-old boys from Amarillo, Otho and Author. The breakfast was of the kind which makes my mouth water to think of it. There was milk, eggs, pancakes, steak, and white bread and butter. The round up for calf branding commenced that day. Otho and Author ate fast; they were excited, for today they were going to help brand, and that is something that not very many American boys get the privilege of doing. Breakfast over we went to the coral, saddled our horses and started to ride some fifteen miles to the point of the first round up.

I rode with Author, Otho and Iry. Iry's outfit was typical cowboy in every way. His saddle was the regulation heavy horn type with a lasso on the horn. Iry's face was mighty brown from wind and sunshine, but on his hands he wore gloves which kept them whiter than my own. Iry rode the saddle with no bounce even at the trot. He carried the reins loosely and guided merely by the pressure of the reins on the horse's neck. His horse, like most cow ponies, was rather small, thin and tough, without a superfluous amount of beauty. We rode slowly along. I asked Iry what pasture we were in.

"Oh," he said, "we're in a little horse pasture up near the quarters." The little horse pasture contained 640 acres.

By asking plenty of questions I got Iry to point out to me some of the interesting features as we rode along. He told me that the little bushes which were dotted everywhere over the rolling plain were mesquite brush. A mesquite bush looks like a locust tree. It's a true legume with locust like leaves and pods. When the cattle are hard up they eat the tender shoots of the brush. All over the plains were scattered what we call Spanish Bayonette, but what Iry called Mexican Soapweed.

Iry told me that they had had a big rain a couple of months before and that was the first they had had for nearly six months.

"You see," he said, "the big rains come along in April, May and June, and the pasture's way up high by this time and the cattle are looking fine. This year and last, tho', rains have been scarce, and pasture's been short, and our cattle's been thin. They are just as 'pore as snakes' now and ain't noway in the shape they ought to be at this time of year."

We had passed beyond the little 640-acre horse pasture and were on the edge of the big 100,000-acre pasture. The plains on one side of us rolled down to the river; on the other side they rose higher and at times broke out into big red hills gashed with gullies and bare of vegetation. As Iry expressed it, "those hills are not worth a _____."

Besides the mesquite brush and soapweed there was a scattering of very short grass. This was mostly mesquite and gramma grass. It was short and not very green, but it makes fine pasture when there are anywhere near enough rains.

We urged our horses to a gallop. After a short time we came to a gate near which were two cowboys with a bunch of ten or twelve loose horses. These were part of the remuda and the two cowboys wanted Iry to take them over to the new camp. Most of the horses which the cowboys ride are merely pasture fed. They are not hard enough to stand a whole day's riding on their scanty feed, so an extra string of horses called the remuda are kept on hand. They are turned loose to graze, but it is one man's duty (the horse wrangler's) to watch them. At noon, when the cowboys want a change of horses, the remuda is run into a little roped in space. Each man ropes a fresh horse and the rest of the remuda is turned out to graze until the next day.

So, it was that Iry had to take part of the remuda over to the horse wrangler at the camp for which we were bound. The horses were let through the gate, they started off at a mad gallop, Iry started after them, and they disappeared over a rise of ground. Otho, Author and I galloped on steadily and came onto them fifteen minutes later. Iry's horse was trotting along slowly and the remuda was strung out in a string behind following. We stayed discreetly in the rear for fear of frightening them.

In this manner we trotted along steadily for several miles, [and] I tried to take in the plains scene. It is hard to describe; it's so big and broad and monotonous. The mesquite covered plains roll up and down and on and on till they strike a bunch of ragged, bare red hills which are cut by the water into steep bluffs and jagged ravines. That was about all I could see to it except the general air of vastness which can't be described.

With the exception of a few young Hereford steers in the distance we saw few cattle. The country for the most part seemed as wild as though man had never been there. Once in five, ten or fifteen miles there is a good barbed wire fence. We saw three or four windmills on our trip. This is the way water is provided for the cattle almost entirely. There is plenty of wind and the big steel tanks are easily kept full.

The Chuck Wagon

Along about 10 o'clock we climbed over a rise of ground and Author pointed out the "chuck" wagon to me. The "chuck" wagon is the camp. On it is carried the grub and the rolls of bedding.

To the right of the "chuck" wagon was a big bunch of cattle and a couple of cowboys were bringing a lot over the hill beyond. The bunch was big, broad, squirming and shifting. There was a constant bawling of lost calves and bereft mothers. A calf would straggle behind its mother; then the mother would look around wildly for her baby, and lock horns with the nearest cow. Meanwhile the calf would come running up again and all would be well with

194

this particular family. But this was going on over the whole herd and as a consequence the bunch didn't move very fast.

Iry had delivered his horses to the wrangler and we helped the boys drive the rest of the cattle to the corral. Most of the boys had been out since daybreak rounding the cattle out of the ravines and draws. We were just in on the finish. When we got nearly to the corral Iry advised me to go over to the "chuck" wagon and rest a bit. I was sorry to leave the finish, but knowing that I would probably be in the way I rode over to the wagon. Here I met Cruz, the Mexican cook. He showed where to get a drink from a cask hung on the shady side of the wagon. That water was murky. If a dollar were put in the bottom of a cup of it there wouldn't be much seen of the dollar. Added to this it was warm.

But, though that water was as warm as dishwater and soupy in appearance, I didn't stop until I had consumed five cups of it. Cruz told me: "No very good water, we get better tomorrow."

My dryness satisfied, I looked around a bit to see just what sort of a place a "chuck" wagon was and what sort of a man was Cruz, the Mexican cook and lord and master of the grub.

The "chuck" wagon was like a camper's wagon, covered with canvas. Out behind the wagon the canvas was carried and was held up with a pole at each corner. This made a shady spot to the rear. Right under the rearmost part of the canvas the fire was built in a little trench, at either end of which was placed an iron stake, and resting on these

A cowboy with Murdo Mackenzie, manager of the Matador Land and Cattle Company, whose Alamositas Ranch was visited by Henry A. Wallace (Archives for the American Southwest, Texas Tech University; 1909 photograph)

stakes and parallel with the ground was an iron bar from which hung hooks over the fire. On these hooks hung kettles of coffee, beans, stew and potatoes. At one side was a covered kettle with embers on top the cover; the biscuits were baking.

I sat down in the shade under the canvas and talked to the cook as he moved around seasoning and stirring his concoctions over the fire. Cruz was short and wide with broad, squat features. His dark brown leathery looking face was continually cracked by a good natured smile. I judged that Cruz was a lot more Indian than Spanish.

"Hot today," said Cruz. "You tired, pretty soon you get sleepy. Better lay down under wagon and take a sicsta."

I was completely contented; the stew simmered lazily; Cruz moved back and forth quietly, talking softly; my head wobbled and I was well started on a delicious doze when in came the horse wrangler to get a drink and talk with Cruz. He squatted down in the shade, rolled his cigarette and commenced to discuss local news. Whether or not he was trying to impress me I don't know, but he talked of shootings and cuttings and as he talked of each case he would try and fix the blame and show where each man made his mistake.

"The men in the panhandle are just as ornery as they ever was," he said, "but the laws are getting so strict that they are afraid to cut up like they used to."

I dozed off to sleep and then awoke with a jerk when a bunch of cowboys rolled in for dinner. I crawled out from under the wagon and watched them. They tied their horses by winding their reins around a mesquite bush two or three times. Then they came up to the "chuck" wagon and joshed Cruz. Otho and Author and a few of the men washed their hands and then Cruz called, "All ready, boys," and a wild scramble occurred. Each man hurried to grab a tin plate, knife, fork, spoon and a cup. I saw it wasn't the place for company manners and so wasn't the last man to get equipped. It was lunch served cafeteria style. I stopped at the stew and ladled out a bit; sampled the beans and potatoes; helped myself to a couple of biscuits; but shied at the coffee.

Each man squatted where he could find the ground and pitched in. Otho, Author and myself sat on a roll of bedding at the side of the wagon. The stew would, I suppose, hit the Mexican palate about right, but it struck me as pretty hot stuff. In spite of the peppery seasoning, I didn't hesitate to get the best of it. Considering the materials, the cooking was fine, but if I were going to have a couple of weeks of such a diet I would want plenty of horseback riding to help my digestive organs. Soon we were through; each man scraped off his plate carefully to avoid anger from the cook, and piled it in the dish pan.

Otho told me that last year he had forgotten once to scrape his plate and put it in the dish pan. The next meal Cruz put salt in his coffee; and Otho never forgot again.

Otho and Author, the city boys, are sons of two of the richest men of Amarillo. For several years they have spent a part of their vacation on the ranch. Before this year they have been too small to help much, but this year they were looking forward to the branding with great relish.

Said Otho, "Old man Mitchell says we can 'rassle' calves this afternoon. I bet I can throw the biggest one they bring in."

Branding the Calves

Dinner over, the cowboys didn't wait for any after dinner nap, but changed horses and rode over to the corral where the cows and calves were now penned up. In one corner of the corral was a hot fire and in it were the branding irons warming up for the afternoon's work.

It was very warm; the sun beat straight down on the dusty corral with its thick, squirming mass of bawling red cattle. Many anxious cow mothers were pushing back and forth in the packed mass to find lost babies.

Then work began; two cowboys rode into the mass swinging their lassos; each roped a calf and galloped in with his victim to near the branding fire. The calf trailed along behind, bawling and jumping and kicking. Otho and Author had the privilege of "rasslin' " the first calf, so out they rushed. Otho grabbed the calf under the neck and by the rear flank, gave a heave, and in a trice the calf was on its right side. Author grabbed the calf's right leg and, sitting down, held it firmly, bracing himself against the calf's left leg. Then the man with the brand got busy; he put a 9 on the shoulder to show the year the calf was born and the company brand, a sort of a V, on the thigh. The branding looked simple; the man holds the hot iron by its long handle in both hands; then putting one foot on the calf he presses down firmly. There's a smoke of burning hair and the branding's over, but that's not all. Along comes Mr. Mitchell and cuts the end of the calf's ear off and if he is a male makes a steer out of him.

Otho and Author were mighty proud of the way in which they had handled their first calf, but they weren't so lucky on their next one. He was a big fellow and the rope slackened up a bit before Otho could get to him. Otho reached for his neck and flank and gave a heave, but the calf gave a squirm, Otho fell down and the calf on top of him. The cowboys gave him yells of encouragement. "Stay by him, Otho; don't let him go. Which is boy and which is calf? I'm betting on the calf." Finally Otho and Author won out and the calf was turned loose a minute or two later considerably less frisky. Otho and Author stayed in the game for half an hour or so and then sat down by the fence to watch the cowboys do the work.

The whole operation of roping, branding and cutting a calf is done a whole lot quicker than I can tell it. In comes the calf bawling and jumping (about six seconds); then it's thrown on its side (about three seconds); then the branding's done (about ten seconds); and at the same time the foreman's using the knife on the calf's ear. Poor calf! Seeing this performance three or four times wounds a man's sensibilities considerably. When it's seen twenty or thirty times feelings become well calloused over. The calf doesn't seem to mind it so very much. It bawls pretty lustily till the iron touches and then quiets down a bit as a rule, although some bawl louder than ever. All hold their mouths wide open, loll their tongues out and get them covered with dust.

The smell of burning hair and hide, the look of anguish in the big calf eyes, the continual bawling, the dusty atmosphere and the hot sun make the corral what might be called rather a disagreeable place. I thought so for about half an hour. Then getting used to the scene I wanted to help, and got the privilege of dumping the calves over on their sides. It's pretty good exercise and I got to enjoy the branding more.

The boys who handle the calves as they come in have quite a bit of sport. When a big one comes in raising a tremendous fuss there's a bit of competition to see who will get a chance. When a big one comes in raising a fuss it is pretty dirty work, but I thought it was the most fun of any part of the branding. At first the boys were inclined to make a good bit of fun of their new hand. I made breaks all right and they enjoyed them, but after a short time I got to handling the calves pretty easily as they came in, although a frisky one now and then would give some rough and tumble work. We worked steadily for an hour and a half and then stopped to give the ropers' ponies a rest. One of the boys counted the tips of the calves' ears which Mr. Mitchell had stuck in his pocket after cutting them off. One hundred and ten calves had been branded.

Then work came on again; unbranded calves were getting scarcer and it was taking the boys longer to rope them. Calves would come in roped in every possible way; around the neck was commonest; some were roped around the body, some on the fore feet, others on the hind feet, and others in combinations of these ways. Work kept on until about 4 o'clock, when we had run out of calves. Two hundred and fifty-one had been branded that afternoon in less than three hours.

The corral gate was opened and the cows and calves were turned back into the pasture. For several days the calves will be sore from branding and won't move very far; about 95 per cent of them live.

There was a bunch of yearling heifers which was not

Branding calves at Alamositas (Archives for the American Southwest, Texas Tech University)

turned out but was kept in the corral until it could be transferred to another pasture the next day.

Some of us who had nothing to do went over to the "chuck" wagon to wait for supper. Around the wagon a lot of bedding was being sunned to dispose of the "varmints." Mr. Mitchell told me the tale of the bedding which I was to have that evening.

"Let me see," he said, "Ed had that bed about two weeks ago; he noticed their biting right considerable, but he didn't know what it was. At last he caught one of 'em and showed it to another of the boys, who talked to him something like this: 'You blamed fool, that's a grayback and the biggest one I ever seen, too!' The fool found he was just lousy with them."

Mr. Mitchell quieted down my fears considerably by

saying that he had got some new bedding since and had aired it "right regular."

Supper passed off in the same style as dinner. Supper over, Otho, Author and I went down to take a look at the Canadian river, a half a mile or so away. It was up and carrying clay to beat the Missouri. As I looked at the water I wanted a swim, and after the dusty day at the corral I decided that the water couldn't make me any dirtier. Otho felt the same way about it, but Author was tired and stood on the bank and laughed at us as we plunged into the murky river. We came out completely covered with red sediment. We needed whisk brooms rather than towels. When we got back to camp the boys were inclined to be facetious and took turns inquiring, "How's the water, boys?"

The sun was just going down, but the boys were arranging their bed rolls on the ground. Otho, Author, myself and three or four of the boys sat down and talked for awhile. Otho and Author were great favorites with the boys.

I tired of their talk, wrapped the blankets around me and slept, despite the fact that the yearling heifers were bawling steadily in the corral. All night long I vaguely knew that they were still bawling. We had a 4:30 breakfast and work began. The cowboys started out to round up the cows and calves on the other side of the river. By 10 o'clock they had routed out a big bunch. There was no corral this time and five or six cowboys had to hold the shifting mass while the rest roped calves, "rasseled" and branded them. Work goes on smoothly except for the rushes of some frantic mother to escape from the bunch. The boys hold the 200 or 300 cows almost perfectly and soon we have 200 calves' ears' tips. This is all in this bunch.

We go back to the "chuck" wagon for dinner. The boys have branded most of the calves in this neighborhood and that afternoon the "chuck" wagon is to be shifted eight or ten miles further on. All the calves in this neighborhood will be branded and then another shift till all the ranch is covered.

This is a general example of the way they did the branding. It is sure a wide, open, outdoor life, but comforts are nil and many things which we call necessities in Iowa are not there at all. When the time came to drive back to the ranch headquarters I was not altogether sorry to see a bit of civilization again.

The ranch house is very pretty. Around it are vines, flowers, roses and locust trees. Accommodations in every way are right up with our most modern improvements. Very few farm homes in Iowa can equal it. Not the least of the improvements, in my estimation, was a beautifully clean porcelain bath tub. By means of this I got rid of the crust of Canadian river mud and corral dust. Within two hours of the time I hit the ranch house I looked and felt a different being. A good bath, a shave and clean clothes heighten one's respect for one's self immensely. Then I was in shape to appreciate properly the ranch house supper, with its thick, juicy steak, its fresh milk and eggs, its corn bread and light bread, its best of lemon pie and cake, and its fruit.

Breeding Herefords

The next morning I rode five miles from the ranch house to see the pure bred Hereford herd. This is kept to supply the bulls, or rather help supply them, needed for grading up the range stock. About 100 head of pure bred Herefords composed the herd. It is evident that the foundation stock has been most carefully selected. Mr. Plimmons, the manager, thinks a lot of the herd bull, Strike Eight. When I saw him he was weighing up around 2200. He was shown at the Denver show last year and came out with second prize, and there were not a few who thought he should have had better. He is of fine Hereford type, close to the ground, with a wide spring of the ribs, and covered with thick flesh. A two-year-old bull, Dode, is much of the same type, and Mr. Plimmons had a yearling coming on which is an exceptionally strong one, good enough to set a hot pace for most of the crack yearlings of the corn belt. The herd of breeding matrons contains representatives from most of the leading herds of the country. The foundation stock was bought at the different live stock shows and sales, without very much regard to price so long as the quality was secured. Mr. Plimmons takes special pride in his bunch of yearling heifers. I had not expected to see such an excellent bunch of young stuff down here. With the foundation stuff to start with and the careful attention paid to herd bulls, there is no reason why this breeding herd should not continue to improve. It is more difficult to develop a high class pure bred herd in the range country than in the corn belt, for the man who is breeding for the range must keep in mind all the time the absolute necessity of ability to forage and rustle. Without this an animal on the range would be short-lived. The Herefords are popular in this section. The tendency to become peaked behind and to decrease in size is corrected occasionally by a judicious cross of one or two Short-horn bulls.

The typical steer looks like a high grade Hereford. The markings are Hereford. The steers on the Alamositas ranch average much above the common range steer. A load of steers from this ranch won the grand championship at the American Royal Show at Kansas City this fall.

The range furnishes a big outlet for Hereford bulls. Last year the Matador Land and Cattle Company bought some $10,000 worth and the year before about $12,000 worth. Other big ranches in the southwest draw heavily from the northern Hereford herds.

The Alamositas ranch is owned by the Matador Land and Cattle Company, the manager of which is Murdo MacKenzie, well known throughout the entire stock country. The company owns an 800,000-acre ranch in the southern panhandle, the 250,000 acres in this northern panhandle ranch, a large ranch in North Dakota and another in Saskatchewan, Canada. The southern ranch is really a large breeding ranch and from this the yearlings are moved north to be finally finished off in the Dakotas and Canada. The mild winters make the northern panhandle a fine breeding location, but the heat and rather sparse grass make conditions less favorable for fitting the cattle for market than in the north.

I thoroughly enjoyed my visit to the Alamositas ranch. It showed me a sight of American cattle business with which Iowans are but little familiar. While the panhandle is settling up in some sections, much of it will never be fit for anything but cattle range.

⪧ XIII ⪦

The Reclamation Act

Of all the acts which Roosevelt stood behind, the Reclamation Act passed by congress June 17, 1902, will probably be thought most of by the western people fifty years from now. The work which the government is now doing because of this act will water nearly 3,000,000 acres of land. Land which in its natural state produces practically nothing and is worth next to nothing, under the touch of the government engineer will be worth from $80 to $2,500 an acre. Land which formerly could support only a few scattering families will, when irrigated, support a family to every eighty acres or less. It is often said that an acre of irrigated land is worth two acres of our best land in the rain watered east. The soil is richer in mineral plant food than our humid soils, water can be provided just when it is needed, and sunshine is more abundant. Irrigated land is ideal for intensive farming of every sort, especially for fruit raising. Irrigation means that there will be from two to six times as many farmers on a quarter section as there is on our humid land. This means in many respects ideal farming conditions; central schools, co-operative marketing, good roads, improved conveniences, and better social conditions. An old English writer once made a remark to the effect that a man who made two

Note: Chapter 13, "The Reclamation Act," was published in *Wallaces' Farmer,* December 31, 1909.

blades of grass grow where one grew before did more than the whole race of politicians. The government reclamation act is doing a far greater work; it is providing for two families where there were none before. The 3,000,000 acres which the government is now watering would support at least 200,000 people.

Some people argue that there was no need of the government taking up the work of irrigation, that private corporations can and are doing the work just as well. The objection is ill founded, for the government in almost every case has tackled those propositions which were too big for any private corporation to handle. In this way the government is irrigating millions of acres of land which could not have been reached for years to come save through the strong arm of the government.

The reclamation act is simple and wise in its provisions; it is made to benefit the people as a whole and not any one class. It provides that all the money got from the sale of public land in sixteen of the western states and territories shall be set aside as a special fund, to be known as the reclamation fund, which is to be used to irrigate land in those sixteen states and territories. It is the secretary of interior's business to execute the law, and when he finds upon examination by his engineers that it is practical to irrigate a certain tract of land he withdraws such land from entry until he is sure just how much of the land it will be advisable for the government to irrigate. Then, having decided that a given project is practicable, the secretary of interior may let contracts for the construction of irrigation works, provided that there is available sufficient money in the reclamation fund. He must then give public notice of how much land is going to be irrigated, of the maximum acreage which one man can homestead on, the probable cost per acre of the water, and how long the owners of the land may have to pay this cost. The government constructs the irrigation works, and the owners of the land pay for them at cost in ten annual payments without interest. Homesteading on land under a government reclamation project is much the same as any other homesteading, but a residence of five years is required in all cases, and before patent may be obtained for the land the government water right must be paid for in full and at least one-half of the irrigable land must be reclaimed. One interesting clause of the act provided that no man under a government project shall own more than 160 acres under the penalty that the government will not furnish water to the surplus acreage.

Seven years ago this act was passed and now there are twenty-nine different projects representing the investment of something like $50,000,000 and covering nearly 3,000,000 acres of land in the states and territories of Arizona, California, Idaho, Kansas, Montana, Nebraska, Nevada, New Mexico, North Dakota, Oregon, South Dakota, Utah, Washington and Wyoming. The government is putting water on the fertile soil of these projects at a cost varying from $22 an acre on the Minidoka project in Idaho to $60 an acre on the Umatilla project of Oregon.

From the Rio Grande project in southern New Mexico to the St. Mary project in northern Montana it is 1,000 miles, and from the North Platte project in western Nebraska to the Orland project in California it is 800 miles; yet the conditions on of all this land which the government is irrigating are wonderfully the same in the crops which it produces. Everywhere alfalfa, sugar beets, small grains and orcharding are a success. The Salt river valley of Arizona may take pride in her oranges, while the Yakima valley projects of Washington specialize in winter apples, yet on all the projects north or south, east or west, a type of farming as intense and a farm civilization as high as any which has yet been seen on this continent will spring up. On many of these projects all of the land which the government is planning to irrigate is at present in private hands, but on many more of them land can be got practically for nothing under the terms of the homestead law.

The work which the government had done on many of the projects is little short of marvelous. Down in Arizona water will be stored up by a dam 284 feet high, and water will be used to water 200,000 acres of land, a large part of which would be a sand desert without it. On the Minidoka project of southern Idaho the barren sage brush desert of a few years ago is changed now by the government into land which is worth more, acre for acre, than our corn belt land. One of the most brilliant projects is that of the Uncompahgre valley of western Colorado, which President Taft opened a few months ago. This project was only made a thing of reality by the daredevil survey of some government engineers and the hard, careful work of bringing the water of the Gunnison river six miles by tunnel through a range of mountains and then spreading it out over the desert of the Uncompahgre valley.

Under Roosevelt's administration, Secretary of Interior Garfield was largely responsible for the great growth of the reclamation service. At present there is a great deal of speculation as to whether Secretary Ballinger of the present administration will continue expanding the work which former Secretary Garfield started. The tendency as shown by Taft's speech at Spokane a couple of months ago will be for a much more conservative growth of the reclamation service. He pointed out that formerly the strict letter of the law had not been lived up to and that many projects had been started when there was not sufficient money in the reclamation fund to complete them. The danger from this course, he shows, is due to the fact that the homesteaders on a government project are practically helpless until water is delivered. The fact that water has not yet been delivered does not excuse a homesteader from living out the full five years, and if projects are started when the funds are not available to complete them, there is great danger that the watering of a project will be delayed and men who have staked their all on a government project will suffer. To overcome this difficulty President Taft recommends that the coming congress authorize the secretary of the interior to issue bonds to the value of $10,000,000. President Taft expresses himself as wonderfully impressed with the marvelous productivity of irrigated land and overwhelmed by the need for further irrigation. But at the same time he evidently believes that in the past the reclamation service has been over enthusiastic.

It is to be hoped that the present administration by its conservatism will not stifle the great work which the reclamation service has so grandly started. May the reclamation fund, renewed every ten years, continue during the rest of this twentieth century redeeming the desert land of the west until the entire water supply has been used. In that day the arid west will be as important in its productivity and its civilization as the humid east.

The Corn Belt Farmer in the Irrigated Country

The Soil of the Arid West

Last summer, while traveling in the west, I was strongly impressed by the difference in the soil type of the humid and the arid states. The first thing which surprised me about western soils is their light color. A great majority of the soils of the arid west range from a light yellow to a gray buff. The reason for this difference in color is easily found. If you break up the rock from which all soils are mainly formed and powder it, you would have a yellow, gray or buff colored dust. Now if you add a lot of leaf mold and dead grass to this powder and let the mixture stand for a long time, the color will be changed to a dark brown or black. This shows the reason why the western soils are so light in color; they lack humus. While our humid soils have been growing grasses for thousands of years to make their color dark brown or black, the dry western soils have had only enough water to grow but very little plant growth, and as a result they are just about the same color now as when the rock broke down to form them.

From the first glance which I had at western soils, it seemed to me as though the western soil must be a joy to work, as compared with our heavy, black prairie soil. Most

Note: The section "The Soil of the Arid West" was published in *Wallaces' Farmer,* January 21, 1910.

of the arid soils seem to be rather sandy and open in texture. The reason for this is the fact that the western soils have not been frozen, beaten upon by the water, and carried around by the winds for as many tens of thousands of years as have the soils of the central states. In other words, the process of disintegration has not been carried on as long, and the result is that the particles of the arid soil are much larger and don't stick together as tightly. Our eastern clays are examples of soils where disintegration has gone so far and the particles have become so fine that they stick together almost like cement and make what we call a heavy soil. One big advantage of the open soil is that it can be cultivated very soon after it becomes wet without injuring the physical condition. This point is rather a revelation to the humid region farmer, who can't get onto a field for sometimes days after a rain. There is one kind of clay to be found in the arid west which is usually called adobe. Adobe is found quite commonly in parts of Idaho and California, and causes lots of trouble until it has been cultivated a few years and made to become less like cement.

But the most interesting difference that I could see between the western soils and those of our humid states is the fact that the western soil is usually more productive if water is added. The reason here is a little harder to find but it is plain to the chemists; arid soils have been rained on but very little, and the result is that nearly all the fertility that was in the original rock is still in the soil. None has been washed into the sea to be lost forever. Our humid soils have been leached by the rains of thousands of years, and millions of tons of their best fertility have been carried to the ocean.

213

Analyses of western soils show that they are far richer than humid soils in phosphorus and potassium, and besides this phosphorus and potassium of the western soil is for a large part in a soluble form, while that of the humid soil is mostly insoluble, the soluble phosphorus and potassium being dissolved by rains and washed out. This solubility of plant food is a very important point, for plants can't use a particle of plant food until it is in soluble form. But although the arid soil is immensely superior to our humid soil in containing such a lot more soluble phosphorus and potassium, at the same time our humid soils almost always contain more nitrogen. Now plants must have a plentiful supply of nitrates, as well as phosphorus and potassium. For this reason arid soils, before they become most productive, must have alfalfa grown on them to bring nitrogen from the air and put it in the soil. Supply water and add nitrogen and humus by growing alfalfa, and you have in the arid soil of the west one of the most productive soils in the world.

The Corn Belt Farmer in the Irrigated Country

Can corn belt men become irrigation farmers in a short time? Scattered over the west are many Iowa, Illinois, Missouri, Kansas, Nebraska and Minnesota men who have become successful irrigators in the space of a year or two, but they made mistakes and will make more of them before they become entirely familiar with the ins and outs of irrigation farming. There are lots of things which the man

Note: The section "The Corn Belt Farmer in the Irrigated Country" was published in *Wallaces' Farmer,* March 11, 1910.

from the humid country who wishes to irrigate must learn either from experience or advice; the latter is much the cheaper. In any irrigated community there are some men who by long practice have become thoroughly familiar with the best methods of handling water under local conditions of climate, soil, etc. The advice of these men, when it can be got, is valuable, but there are general rules of clearing, leveling, laying out laterals, and applying water, which apply to a large part of the western irrigated country.

The one thing important above all others is the water right. Most western land without water is worth practically nothing; with water, it is worth anywhere from $80 to $200, or even more, an acre. The first thing then is for the would-be irrigator to be absolutely sure that his water right is assured and unfailing. There are many ways of getting water to irrigate land; one farmer may take it directly from a stream. The government furnishes the most absolutely certain water supply; some private companies may furnish just as good water rights, but a rain belt farmer cannot feel sure about them, as to their priority of water right, water rights sold, amount of water allowed for irrigation each season, general efficiency and permanency of the canal structures. The government canal structures are all of them most permanent, and an abundance of water is always assured. This is not always the case with private companies; for instance, this past summer in southern Idaho the ditch of a private company running along a side hill, broke, and before the water could be shut off a great hole was washed out. After several weeks the damage was repaired and the water was turned on again, but the work had been done imperfectly, and the canal again washed out. The result of this trouble was disastrous to the people under the ditch; for a month and more they could get no water. Crops withered before their eyes, alfalfa turned brown and dry, the apple and prune trees commenced to suffer. To see this made the people writhe in anger; it wasn't through Providence that their crops were suffering; it was because of the blunders of a canal company.

In the Salt River valley of Arizona there were formerly many private canal companies, but there was not water enough to go around, and the consequence was that in a dry season the land under the latter companies went unwatered, and the crops died and the land went back to the desert.

Above everything else, the eastern farmer must know just exactly what he is getting for a water right.

When it comes to the actual preparation and irrigation of land, there are lots of important things to know, but the first and foremost is the necessity for reducing land to a level, uniform grade. In western Kansas, in Arizona, in California, in southern Idaho, everywhere in the irrigated west, practical irrigators lay prime importance upon having the land level, that is, on a smooth, uniform grade. Crops depend upon getting water, and unless the land is leveled well it is a tremendous job to distribute water evenly. Extra expense put on leveling the land in the first place is repaid later ten or one hundred fold. It costs anywhere from $3 to $15 an acre or more to plow, harrow and properly level with a buck scraper. It takes a careful eye, and if the work is to be done right, a civil engineer should really be employed to run levels.

On a large share of the western land before it can be

leveled the native growth of sage brush, mesquite, or whatever it may be, must be taken off. This will cost anywhere from practically nothing to $5 to $6 an acre. Sage brush is usually got out of the way by grubbing or dragging across it both ways with railroad irons.

After clearing and leveling has been done, the next thing in order is to locate the field laterals. Here again it is best to put an engineer to work with his level. After he has located them, they may be made with a common walking or lister plow.

There are several different general methods of getting the water on to the land. The commonest are the check method, the furrow method, and the flooding from field ditches. The check method is used almost entirely in Arizona and California. This consists in dividing a field to be irrigated into plots or checks of an acre or two each, which are bounded by earthen levees of dirt. To throw up these levees in the first place is quite expensive, costing from $7 to $20 an acre to get a field in shape. An engineer is almost essential to locate the checks and ditches. But after the levees are thrown up and a good head gate is put in the bank of each check, this method is one of the most convenient by which to get water on the land. It is mainly a matter of opening head gates and letting the water flow; one man can water seven to fifteen acres a day. The check method is especially adapted to level slopes, sandy soils, and big heads of water. On steep slopes or with clay soils checking is not good. Two of the big disadvantages of checking are that the checks are hard on the machinery which must pass over them, and a large amount of surface soil must be removed to make the checks.

In eastern Oregon and southern Idaho a kind of irrigation called the furrow method is practiced. Field laterals are run across the slope ever 300 or 400 feet. Running down the slope from the field laterals every eighteen inches or two feet are furrows three or four inches wide and deep. This method is very good for root crops and orchards, but it is also used for small grains and alfalfa. It uses a small head of water economically, and after the system is well established requires very little attention. This method is especially good for clay soils, which are liable to bake, but for sandy soils is not so good, as the water is liable to soak in the upper end of the furrow and the lower is apt to suffer. The great big trouble with this method is the difficulty of connecting the furrows to the field lateral. The ideal is to put lath boxes or some similar tube in the bank of the ditch every several feet, and then bring several furrows to a head at each box. Then when the water is checked up, it flows out of these boxes and divides among the furrows, and the land is quite evenly watered, with but little care on the part of the irrigator. In practice, however, it is quite common to use no lath boxes to distribute water among the furrows, but simply to divide the water between furrows by constant and careful work with a shovel. This is a long, tiresome, puttering job. The furrow method is ideal for using small but continuous heads of water on rather stiff soils.

The cheapest method, and the one used most through Utah and Colorado is flooding from field ditches. It is well adapted to most crops, but takes a great deal of labor to get the water distributed at all evenly. A good day's work for one man is about three acres. Field laterals are run from the head ditch every 75 or 100 feet on a grade of one-half to three-fourths of an inch to the rod. Irrigation is done by checking up the water in these laterals by canvas, earthen or wooden dams every 75 to 150 feet, and thus making the water overflow from low places in the sides of the bank. To evenly water a field takes lots of watching and careful work with a shovel. Some men who have had long practice, or who are naturally very observing, acquire what is known as the waterer's eye; that is, they have come to know just how the water is going to flow under certain circumstances. These men often hire out at advanced wages to new comers as expert irrigators.

Each crop has its own peculiar requirements in the way of irrigation, and it takes a man some time to learn to meet them. The young alfalfa plant, for instance, should be started out with plenty of moisture in the soil, but shouldn't be watered for some time, in order to make it throw out a deep root system in its search for moisture. The usual custom is to irrigate alfalfa once for each crop; some watering just before cutting, and some just after, the object being to keep the plant growing vigorously all the time. There is a great deal to learn about just where, when and in what quantities to put on the water. Even in the west there are very few men who have mastered irrigation. There is lots of water lost and crops hurt by irrigating too often and too shallowly, by turning the water on for a long time without attending to it, by putting water on land which was not leveled rightly, by not enough cultivation, or by clogged ditches.

The eastern man going into the irrigated west to farm should know what sort of water right he is getting and something of the general principles of irrigation, but he should also investigate soil conditions. There are two soil conditions that must especially be watched for: adobe and alkali. Adobe is a stiff clay-like soil which is very hard to handle till it has been worked for several years. Alkali is the bane of irrigation. Some soils are alkalied before irrigation, but most of them become so because of irrigation. In the west there are many barren acres of alkali waste today which not many years ago were extremely productive. Water applied to crops raised the ground water on the lower levels, and this water, carrying in solution the salts of the upper ground, when it evaporated left a coating of salt on the surface. This coating, called alkali, will not permit the growth of our ordinary cultivated plants. The only cure for alkali is drainage, and it is only a question of time till nearly all irrigated land will be drained to protect it from alkali. Of all the dangers to irrigated land, lack of drainage is the greatest.

If a man has a good water right, if his soil is neither alkali nor adobe, and if he has some knowledge of irrigation conditions, he stands a good chance of succeeding. Besides this, before an eastern man starts in to make a home in the irrigated country, he should have at least $2,000, an unlimited amount of pluck, and a desire to learn continually. There are many inconveniences to be borne at present on the typical irrigation project, but on these same projects there will undoubtedly rise in a short time an example of as high a type of farm civilization as the world has yet seen.

❧ XV ❧

Irrigation Farming

Of all the types of farming, irrigation farming is the highest. It takes more brains and produces more results to the acre of ground than any other. Farming by irrigation is more like manufacturing than farming; in either case, the conditions of production after the plant is put in shape are under almost perfect control. But to put irrigable land in the right shape takes the ability of a man who is laying out a factory. The land must be made level, or rather, with a perfectly uniform slope; ditches for carrying the water must be put in just the right place and head-gates for checking up the water in the ditches must be placed just right. Applying water to the land calls for the nicest kind of judgment; when, where, and how much for each kind of crop. Crops are not depending now on Providence for their water supply; if the soil is puddled, if the crops suffer from drouth or are drowned, it is the fault of the irrigator, not the result of Divine Providence.

Irrigation is intensive farming carried to its finest point. The average size of the irrigation farm in the United States is sixt seven acres, and there is a constant tendency for this row smaller. In Utah the common sized farm is twenty to forty acres and in the fruit sections of Colorado

Note: Chapter 15, "Irrigation Farming," was published in *Wallaces' Farmer,* March 18, 1910.

and California a large share of the farms are from five to ten acres. On many of the government irrigation projects forty acres are recognized as the maximum amount needed to support a family and the government will allow no one to hold more than that. All this simply means that the irrigation project of the future will be densely populated, supporting from two to ten times as many people to the quarter section as corn belt land. With thicker settlement go improved social advantages, schools, town conveniences, etc. In the orange district of southern California and the apple district of Grand Valley, Colorado, these advantages are seen most markedly. Here a whole valley of many thousand acres is one big orchard with houses every few hundred yards. With but little trouble neighbors can run over next door to see each other. Of course there is the telephone, rural delivery, daily paper, and good roads. In some places in these furthest advanced communities there is daily grocery and ice delivery with electric lights in the houses and on the porches. Add to all this a beautiful, sunshiny, health-giving climate, and you have a life which may be envied by both the farmer and the city dweller of the humid east.

One of the very nicest things about irrigation is the wonderful power possibilities. Where water is diverted from a river to a canal there is a chance of putting in a turbine and dropping water through it and taking away its power and changing it to electricity. But the water is just as good for irrigation as it was before. And this power which is thus made by the water can be transmitted for miles, hundreds if necessary, over high tension lines. Then it can be used for all the things for which any power can be used: heating and lighting houses, running interurbans, running washing machines, electric cleaners, electric pumps: possibly furnishing power to run electric engines for plowing and harvesting, as is done in Germany. There are all the tremendous possibilities of which we think when the name electricity is mentioned. And electricity is being developed by the thousands of horsepower on a large number of irrigation projects at the present time; down in the Salt River valley of Arizona power is being carried sixty miles across the mountains by high tension to light Phoenix.

Co-operation goes hand in hand with irrigation. This is not because the irrigation farmer is a superior type to start with, believing in community interest and social confidence. On the contrary, he is very independent, but lack of capital and a crying need for water meant co-operation or leave the country. To get water in the first place meant that corporation or co-operation must do the work. Then after obtaining the water it was absolutely necessary to have some sort of water users' organization in order to get equitable distribution. Neighbor must confer with neighbor as to the best time of using water. Deference must be shown between irrigators, one man at times must give way to his neighbors if he is to get along at all in an irrigated country. All this soon develops in even the most independent of men a consideration for the rights of others and a realization of the benefits to be obtained by working together. So it is not surprising that the best examples of co-operation in the United States today are found in the irrigated west.

Down in southern California the principles of co-operation have been applied to the marketing of all their fruit crops. There is the Southern California Fruit Growers' Exchange, a walnut growers' exchange, a grape growers' exchange, etc. In the famous apple growing districts of Hood river, Yakima, and Wenatchee there are notably successful co-operative packing and marketing concerns. In the Grand Valley of Colorado there is an extremely successful marketing co-operation. Of all these the Southern California Fruit Growers' Exchange, handling over $20,000,000 worth of business annually, is the biggest. Practically all these co-operations started due to the hoggishness and short-sighted policy of the commission men in their efforts to get the utmost possible money out of the growers. Prices were forced down till there was no longer profit in raising the crops, and the growers, having no other alternative but leave the country, applied the principles of co-operation which they learned in handling water to the marketing of fruit. These co-operations have been markedly successful and have saved growers millions of dollars. In the corn belt commission men show more judgment and do not push the farmer to the point where in order to live he must co-operate. It might be well for the corn belt farmer if the commission man was more rapacious.

At present conditions are not ideal on most of the irrigated projects. They are very newly settled, present a rather barren appearance, and conveniences are just coming in. Life under pioneering conditions must be endured for several years to come on a large number of projects. Railroads have taken advantage of many of these new communities by charging excessive freight rates. Yet conditions are rapidly changing, and in a few years from now the owner of an irrigation farm will be envied.

Index

Index

Index

Mexicans, as beet field workers: 29, 30–31

Milo maize: 38–39

Miner's inch: 76, 119

Minidoka project (Idaho): 144–57, 159, 209, 210

Moisture storage, in dry farming: 180, 186

N

Nampa country (Idaho): 141–42

New Mexico, homesteading in: 50

Nitrogen: 46, 55, 64, 86, 116, 128, 214

North Plains (Texas): 35–36

O

Olla jars: 59, 63

"On the Trail of the Corn Belt Farmer" (Wallace): 13, 26–34

Orange crops: in California, 79–81, 85–86, 102; in Salt River Valley, 54–57, 58–59, 62, 64, 210

Orchards: see Fruit growing

Ostriches, raising: 60–61

P

Palisades, Colo.: 174–75

Parma, Idaho: 118

Pasture land: 48, 63, 89

Payments, installment, for water usage: 14, 20, 21, 137, 155, 158, 209

Peach orchards: 83, 101

Phoenix, Ariz.: 51 53, 223

Phosphorus: 64, 116, 214

Pioneer Irrigation Company: 133–34

Plainview, Texas: 40–41

Plowing: 43, 182

Potash: 116

Potassium: 214

Potato growing: 150, 178–80

Power house, Roosevelt Dam: 71–72

Private companies: under Carey Act, 141, 144, 158–59, 166–68, 208; and water rights, 133–34, 215–16

Public land sales: 208

Puddling: 132, 221

Pumps: 27, 28, 65, 156

R

Railroads: 45

Rainfall: 99, 105, 127; at Cheyenne, Wyo., 186–87, 189; in Texas Panhandle, 37, 39, 45, 46

Real estate, selling tactics: 45–46, 162–62, 184, 188–89

Reclamation Act (1902): 14, 15, 20, 21–22, 207–11

Reclamation projects: 12, 18, 167–68

Reclamation Service (Department of Interior): 14–15, 17

Red river: 35, 38

Relinquishments: 151–52

Ridenbaugh ditch: 136–37

Roosevelt, Theodore: 6–7, 11, 14, 207, 210

Roosevelt, Ariz.: 70

Roosevelt Dam: 57, 59, 64, 66–77

Roswell, Idaho: 127–29

Rupert, Idaho: 144, il. 146

Russians, as beet field workers: 29, 31

Rye planting: 109–10

S

Sacramento, Calif.: 100–101

Sacramento river: 100

Sacramento Valley, Calif.: 79, 98–103

Sagebrush, clearing of: 109, 116, 125, 137–38, 217

Salt river: 69

Salt River Valley, Ariz.: 50–65, 210, 216, 223

Sand storms: 110–11, 148

San Joaquin Valley, Calif.: 79, 89–98

Schools, central: 174, 207, 222

Second foot: 119

Seeding, in dry farming: 182–83

Sheep: 61, 120, 161, 163

Smudge pots: 169–70, 171

Snake river: 152, 155, 159–60

227